vivian m. **fong**

tricking
the city

an inside story of
municipal
affairs

Table of Contents

Acknowledgements

Everyone says that writing a book is a labor of love and a daunting process. For this particular story, it was also a well-thought tribute. To our son, Josh, who bolstered our cause; to the City of Demorest in which my husband and I have made our home for decades (and for John, generations); to the people who have supported our businesses; to our neighbors and friends who have stood by us during John's foray into city council affairs; and even to those who attempted to recall John's appointment simply because he stood for the truth—all figures, all experiences make us stronger.

Finally, to readers who have never heard of or stepped foot in Demorest, Georgia but found interest in my story. Pursue the truth with all the fire inside of you.

All proceeds from this book will be donated to the Demorest Springs Park renovation project.

Introduction

THE TRUTH ABOUT LOCAL GOVERNMENT

*"A healthy democracy requires a decent society; it requires that
we are honorable, generous, tolerant and respectful."*
—CHARLES W. PICKERING,
ATTORNEY, POLITICIAN, AND JURIST

If you could listen to the heartbeat of a city, you would hear the
constant pounding from traffic, people, rattling of infrastructure, even nature vying for space among the innovative crevices of
humankind. No wonder city dwellers are dreaming in New York
City, sinning in Las Vegas, and falling in love in Paris. Cities are
the pulse of life.

I am a first-generation Asian American from Taipei, Taiwan,
which has a strong heart, with gleaming structures among the tallest
in the world, lightning-speed elevators, and bustling night markets.
My home has been the city of Demorest, Georgia, for decades,
however. Its heartbeat used to be pretty steady, never too fast, yet
sometimes slow. More recently, its chambers are disrupted, dam-
aged, and compromised.

"Call the city cardiologist!" I feel like shouting. My husband
is a doctor, an optometrist, and so is my son, a medical surgeon.

My niece and nephews are also doctors, so I'm comfortable with all things medical and its power to solve so many grave challenges. What I'm not comfortable with is corruption. That's where my tale begins.

If you survey the annual list of "most corrupt cities" (since these days, there is a public list for *everything*), you'll find Baltimore, Chicago, Philadelphia, and other usual suspects. You won't see Demorest. It's not a metropolis. It doesn't have nationwide expectations to rise to. It is a municipality and doesn't have bottomless resources and forward-thinking programs that compete with other cities for research and development dollars. Nevertheless, it's my city. I met my husband of forty years here, and we raised our son in its school system. My fellow citizens are also worth fighting for.

Municipalities are supposed to be a simple operation. It's not the intricate White House! In fact, the White House (WH) employs almost as many as our entire population (1,800 and 1,973 respectively). For six seasons, the character of Frank Underwood (played by Kevin Spacey) in *House of Cards* depicted crafty, wicked revenge games in the WH masqueraded as politics as usual. The story is engrossing, but you won't catch me binging. The themes hit too close to home. You see, my noble husband was elected as a councilman in November 2019. He's been standing on the big, black X inside the house of cards.

Add masks, social distancing, and other oddities in the year of 2020 (like giant murder hornets, venomous caterpillars, the puppy born with green fur, and hungry monkeys taking over a city in Thailand)—you really can't make this stuff up!

To assess my story that primarily takes place in this one loaded year and draw your own conclusions, a brief background on municipal government will help.

Enhanced Power and Peril

National League of Cities defines *municipal government* as the institution created by states to govern-incorporated localities—particularly cities. States grant powers to municipal governments so that they might provide basic services, such as police and fire protection, as well as solve the special problems associated with urban localities: affordable housing, environmental quality, and parking shortages. As with other levels of government, the powers granted to municipalities have increased dramatically over time. However, the expansion of municipal power came only as cities faced new or growing problems, and municipal officials always seemed to lack the authority or means to solve the crises that faced American cities.

According to the US Embassy, which offers a pretty exhaustive repository of American history online, following English political traditions, many cities functioned under special city charters in the colonial era. Other cities retained their town governments, even as they grew quite large. Early municipal governments concerned themselves largely with commercial issues, administering local marketplaces and wharves, and they provided the barest of services to residents, if any at all. While colonial cities often had democratically elected aldermen, colonial governors generally appointed powerful mayors to run municipalities.

By the mid-1700s, resident concerns over crime, public drunkenness, and other moral shortcomings did encourage municipal responses to urban disorder, but municipal governments continued to be a minor force in the late colonial era. America remained predominantly rural, and as late as 1750, only fourteen "municipal governments" existed.

After independence, national democratic trends brought more directly elected mayors and other political reforms. While state governments dominated by rural representatives continued to express concern about potential urban evils, city residents gained more say in choosing those who would govern their cities, and those who governed gradually gained more power to do so. Through the early 1800s, provision of services continued to expand with the establishment of fire companies, school systems, municipal water supplies, and regular garbage collection. Only problems that posed the gravest of threats to cities received sufficient governmental attention. However, with dense concentrations of wooden structures and water supplies with limited pressure, fires posed a continuous threat to American cities. This threat led to a number of reforms, including regulating against wooden buildings, which New York City had done as early as 1776, and the creation of professional fire-fighting forces.

Over 350 years later, the areas of water and sewage are of particular importance to my story because my husband would be the steward of both upon taking a position on city council.

According to Leonard Curry's book, *The Corporate City*, in the early 1800s, New Orleans with its population of about 2,600, was uniquely governed by a Superior Council, inspired by French colonists, for a short time. What this meant was the Superior Council followed the laws of the *Custom of Paris*. In addition to regular governing, the Council acted as investigator, prosecutor, jury, and judge in all civil and criminal matters. Given the tale I am about to tell you, this idea of a "Superior Council" makes me cringe, as our version is bad enough in 2021!

As French writer Jean-Baptiste Alphonse Karr said, "Plus ça change, plus c'est la même chose." (The more things change, the more they stay the same.)

Since its inception, municipal government may be best known not for its accomplishments, but for its corruption. I have an aspirational goal of changing this. Every day, I see evidence of fragmentation and dictatorship, as much as it twists my stomach in knots to say so. It's worse than the state level or national level because the municipality is not under the jurisdiction of the state attorney general. It's like an island in and of itself with one or two individuals running the whole show and thinking they are a superior council. There is a GMA (Georgia Municipal Association), but when you call for advice, they ask, "What does the city attorney say?" My story answers just that. What do you do when your city attorney, in my view, is an unsavory character whose answers are self-serving?

We've been governed by no written rules, just the influence of a couple of figures. So many twist the truth and manipulation and people call that "savvy politics." To me, it's crafty politics. It doesn't matter who lies and tells the truth.

I feel very fortunate to have had Abe Sharony, our attorney and friend of forty years, along for this wild ride in order to provide legal oversight, balance, and fairness. One significant event was the attempt for my husband to be recalled twice within two months for trying to reveal the corrupted mayor and the city attorney who also caused the city to face a RICO (Racketeer Influenced and Corrupt Organizations Act) violation lawsuit filed by the local college. The plain version is that someone wasn't happy with what John did, so a sly citizen started a petition to remove him from office at the next election. The person was a former councilwoman and accused John of violating the Georgia Sunshine Law (also known as Georgia Open Records Act). It wasn't a bright move on her part. In one instance, the recall didn't even last for one week. In both instances, there weren't enough signatures to recall John, an innocent, lawful citizen and servant leader.

I stand by the integrity of this story, with all events being well-documented. Any words not construed as fact is my opinion independent of my husband or any other individual named and described in *Tricking the City*. Also, since we're in the age of content creation and living out loud online, I do provide social media posts—the publication of such commentary does not imply my endorsement of these posts in any way. Some of the language is offensive, even heartbreaking, but it gives a flavor of what citizens are paying attention to and how they are responding publicly, with Demorest in a blurry spotlight.

Draw your own conclusions. The purpose of the book is to serve as an eye opener to the public that Georgia municipalities are legally uncontrollable by the state attorney general and can be abused by corrupted individuals or groups for their own purposes. Whether you want to scoff at the details, write your own version of municipal mayhem, or hug your narrator, it all comes down to one question. Would you want this trickery for your city?

Chapter 1

ELECTED WITH OPEN EYES

"Perpetual optimism is a force multiplier."
—Colin Powell,
65th U.S. Secretary of State

The editor and founder of a quirky website called *Good Guy Swag* poses thirty characteristics that good guys have. Of course, I was curious, so I read through the list. Well, my guy meets all of the characteristics, but you need only be concerned with the following for the story I am about to tell you: honesty, integrity and character, fights against injustice, has good humor and good manners, supports and promotes moral excellence, and seeks peace when possible. Now that we've gotten the Good Guy Meter out of the way, let's proceed.

On November 8, 2019, Lawrence Bridges, the owner of the local coffeeshop across from Demorest City Hall, invited everyone to attend a voting night gathering at his place, Temperance House Fine Coffee, whose lavender latte and stuffed pimento cheese sandwich are all the rage. Let me tell you, it would take more than the top-grade espresso Lawrence provides our city with to get through the year of events detailed in this book!

The weather that day was quintessential seasonal fall with an evening breeze carrying leaves from their original destination and signs of change. I hoped those changes would all be positive.

We were waiting on the results of the city council election for 2020 with Bruce Harkness, a longtime personal injury and civil trial law attorney known in Demorest for winning over $100 million of recovered costs in paid settlements for his clients. He would become county commissioner in the year of 2021. We were also with Nathan Davis, running for a council seat alongside John, Nathan's fiancé, Tracie, and other guests.

Our collective spirit as we waited to hear the news was that we would play a significant role in turning over a dark era in our city.

We weren't the only ones to feel like this. One sunny afternoon in July 2019 as I was examining the recently remodeled exterior wall at John's upcoming eye clinic on Central Avenue, a tall male appeared behind me. "Hey, are you John Hendrix's wife?" I nodded. "I am Nathan Davis, we have the same electrician, Terry."

"Oh, right." I replied.

"I am running for the city council. I know John is, too." I shook his hand and wished him good luck, then had to turn to speak with the remodeling worker.

The next time I saw Nathan Davis was at the October 2019 city council meeting. John and I were both in attendance. That evening, I learned that Nathan was serving on the city's Downtown Development Authority (DDA). The goal of any DDA is to aggressively develop a community to attract and retain businesses and merchants, along with tourism assets whenever possible, so I was impressed that Nathan committed his time and passion to this for Demorest.

Then his face turned grimmer. He expressed his concern about the 2018 Fourth of July concert performed by the country singer

Josh Turner that costed the city $100,000 with only $20,000 worth of tickets sold. The event resulted in a $80,000 loss for the city. "I wanted to clarify certain public perception," said Nathan. "Mayor Austin initiated the event then persuaded the DDA members to vote for the concert. The mayor suggested that Josh Turner was a popular singer. Not only would the city profit from the famous singer by selling his concert tickets. Josh Turner's performance would also help brand the city."

Nathan also expressed his opinion about Joey Homans serving both as the city attorney and as the mayor's personal attorney who defended a civil fraud case against the mayor. "It's a conflict of interest according to the city charter," he stated like a knowledgeable professor. The details of Nathan's concern will be discussed later in the case of Kingwood Water and Sewer Services (KWSS).

Joey Homans barked back, "I can accept the perception, but I had advised the city, the staff, mayor and council at a far reduced rate out of respect of this community, and I can tell you that number one, that's not going to be the case anymore because I can see the respect that is provided back, number two, there had been time when not just in this situation, but I 've had to conflict out because there's a legal conflict."

Joey took the claim personally and reassured the audience there was no conflict. "There was nothing about that litigation that involved the city."

Naturally, the mayor wasted no time to defend his lawyer friend. "Mr. Homans has billed me for his services in the KWSS case and it was extremely substantial." But the mayor did not offer to present the proof of payment for the same attorney fee.

The information from that meeting was more provocative than I could have imagined. On the way home, I said to John, "Nathan was one of the very few people in town that dared to stand up to both Rick Austin and Joey Homans. He may have earned many votes tonight for the upcoming election." John looked very pensive, perhaps deep in thought about the intricacies. He nodded in agreement.

Nathan is a "red." In the state of Georgia, now deemed blue (much to the dismay of so many of our neighbors), the color distinction matters since it became a part of the "New South" as a show of more liberalism upon the highly contentious 2020 U.S. Presidential election and Senate runoffs. Red or blue, Nathan is influential as a master hair stylist and wants to do good. His family has been living in Demorest for years. Having been in the salon business where gossip is an accessory to a new updo, Nathan heard endless complaints about the mayor and current city council over the spraying of hair products. His clients inspired him to run for a seat on the council.

Tracie was the one to first break the news that both John and Nathan had been elected. She had gone to the election board and saw the posting. Everyone cheered in our group except for one of Mayor Rick Austin's friends in the crowd. Armed with the confirmation of this new phase in our life, John and I had to leave to check on my uncle, who was ill at our home.

Bruce chased us down in the parking lot as Nathan and John were exchanging congratulations to each other. He said with a nervous twitch in his face, "This may be the last time we can all gather like this."

Innocently, John said, "We can all go out to eat sometime, can't we?" We enjoy good food and often eating out with friends and family, so his response didn't surprise me.

Bruce replied cautiously, "The three of us cannot gather as a quorum. Remember the Georgia Sunshine Law. No back-door meetings. It says you can gather, but you *cannot* vote on certain issues."

Bruce's message had an ominous tone. Not familiar with the Sunshine Laws, I was already a little impressionable because although I had wanted John to win the council seat, I knew this four-year commitment would bring some limitations to our planned "retirement." For me, that meant traveling to Utah to see the geologic formations and back to Paris, among so many other places, once the world opened up again post-COVID-19. John and I had traveled the world together and there were still many bucket-list stops. John would have to fulfill the duties of community leadership on top of his busy practice as an optometrist. I supported my husband fully. We had always backed one another's endeavors (even the quirky ones) for more than forty years of marriage.

When John first got elected, he was enthusiastic. We invited the mayor, Rick Austin, and his wife, Jennifer, to Chateau Elan for dinner in order to set the stage for mutual success and good will.

After all, Rick's father, the late Dick Austin and John's parents were life-long friends. In fact, the senior Austin was instrumental to John's appointment to serve on the State Board of Optometry in the 1980s.

Chateau Elan is our go-to spot for all occasions that require an elevated experience. It is reminiscent of an exquisite French country estate, and we're not able to regularly travel to France, which we adore. Being forty miles south of Demorest, Chateau is a beacon of pride for north Georgia, known for weekend getaways, corporate retreats, professionally staffed golf and tennis clubs, and a world-class spa. More recently, the opulent chateau where my family has hosted numerous celebrations, like our son's wedding in 2019, has been moonlighting as a Mexican drug lord's house—in the wildly popular Netflix series, *Ozark*, that is!

Dressed in a suit, but without his signature western cowboy hats, Rick appeared to be quite cordial, which opened the door for more pressing dinnertime topics, like the Georgia Sunshine Laws. We also needed to know what's in the water of Demorest, so to speak, since John suspected he would be put in charge of its oversight. "The Sunshine Law was taken very seriously," said Rick, "I had to excuse myself before at occasions where other council members were present."

I laughed, "I see parties at the White House and state affairs swarming with elected officials and staff all the time."

Prior to dinner, I learned via my own research that the Georgia Sunshine Law was established in 2012 and refers to open records and open meetings between "servants of the people." According to Georgia First Amendment Foundation, "a democratic government assumes that those who elect public officials will have free access to what those public officials are doing. Access to government meetings and records provides citizens with the information they need to participate in the democratic process and to insist that government officials are held accountable for their actions. Agencies that are included under the act are:

- Every state department, agency, board, bureau, commission and authority.
- Every county, municipal corporation, school district or other political subdivision of the state.
- Every department, agency, board, bureau, commission, authority or similar body of each such county, municipal corporation or other political subdivision of the state.
- Every city, county, regional or other authority established pursuant to law.

Georgia First Amendment Foundation even states in its description, Justice Brandeis once said, "Sunlight is the best disinfectant." *Cute!* Or "bless his heart," as we say in the South.

It's understandable why Bruce, who is an attorney, had mentioned this to John as a helpful tip since he just became an elected official. Why did Rick also emphasize the importance of this? Had he violated the Sunshine Law? Or did he want John to misstep and perform a violation in order to keep a coverup going?

The topic had an air of mystery and foreboding. John and I are hardcore rule followers as long as the guidelines lead to what is morally right. We're both fiercely loyal and fair people who can sense injustice. Then we're compelled to do something about it.

As gourmet food piled onto our table with a view since the whole staff at Chateau Elan knew us well, John asked the mayor a range of questions regarding the city finances. There had been a long history of public discontent about expenditures and waste of money. This city is small, with a population of 2,000, but it has a high revenue because the city supplies water in surrounding areas in the county. We claim 486 miles of water line. That is its power, and I would quickly learn that is why politicians have eyes on this city as a piece of lean meat for them. The average income in Demorest is not very high, at around $37,000.

Clearly perturbed that John wanted to talk about the city so he knew what to expect for upcoming meetings, Rick vehemently shook his head. The tension in his light blue eyes under wire-rimmed glasses bounced off the wine glass. He sighed, "Everything is fine. The city is in sound financial condition."

Rick didn't realize that we were armed with valuable research. Note that it's simple to visit *government.com* and search for info on your city. Our pressing question was why Demorest, a tiny city of 2.3 square miles with a population of only 2,000, had $10 million in debt?

Rick huffed, "Which website shows this kind of information? I don't believe that is accurate." So, he was already questioning John's integrity and intelligence.

John is more inquisitive than I am when it comes to numbers. In studying optometry, he had to know chemistry, physics, and math, so his brain lights up when numbers and data are in front of him!

Now in the position to inquire about wrongdoing, the fishhook caught hold.

Even as our gracious server brought another reserve bottle from their list of thirty wines produced and bottled onsite, John couldn't stop himself from pressing the matter because he had a treasure trove of data. Chateau Elan makes a bottle of sparkling wine called Sweet Giggles, which we could have used a dose of now. Either Rick would give a satisfactory explanation while he had a chance over a friendly dinner, or John would be obligated to share the surprises more publicly in his debut city council meeting.

As for me, I was trying to ignore my past experiences with Rick and stay focused on John's interests and the well-being of Demorest.

In January 2018, I was building a duplex on a deserted lot down the street from our residence, which was owned by our family trust, and I tried to apply for a building permit with a variance to be part of the paved parking. After the initial meeting with Kristi Williams, the city manager at the time, and Phil Gruver, city building inspector, the application was submitted to the city's planning commission for recommendation to the city council for final approval. Rick was against it and made it so difficult. The application was nearly tabled twice, which would have constituted a denial unknowingly based on the city ordinance had I not objected to it.

At a city council meeting, which are open to the public, Rick uttered the words, "The handshake and 'get things done' day is over," referring to the tone and tenor of Demorest when John's father had been a councilman. I was standing behind the podium after my presentation and Q & A for the council.

"With all due respect, Mr. Mayor," I said, then turned to the audience, "I expect to be treated the same way as other residents alike in the city, no more, and no less." The city council voted unanimously to approve the building permit.

Thirty minutes prior to this meeting, a call came in from one of my tenants, Terry, across the street from the construction site, informing me with, "The fire chief, Ken Ranalli was here in the city's fire truck. He said that he was sent by the mayor." Terry was out of breath as he was speaking.

"The fire chief also said that the Hendrixes are trying to 'use government property for their personal gain', and the mayor wanted him to find a reason, such as public safety, to convince the council not to approve the permit," Terry asserted with disbelief. That evening at the meeting, our general contractor, Lee Anderson, Terry, and several residents around the duplex site came to show their support as the Demorest City Council voted to grant the building permit.

A few days after the building permit was granted, we were driving somewhere out of town, and I saw the mayor's car and Lee Anderson's car parked in front of the construction site of the duplex. "What was he doing there with our contractor?" John asked. We drove past slowly, and they were shocked to see us. Then Rick started to leave. I saw them exchange phone numbers. Lee Anderson gawked at me. I looked at him. The mayor noted the puzzled look, and said, "My back deck needs some repairs so I was asking if Lee could do this work for me."

Since that day and for six months after, no work was ever performed by this contractor, and it was mutually agreed that he resign from the project.

Chapter 2

A CALLING, A CONSCIENCE

"Hope begins in the dark, the stubborn hope that if you just show up and try to do the right thing, the dawn will come. You wait and watch and work: you don't give up."

—ANNE LAMOTT, NOVELIST

IN ADAM GRANT'S captivating and insightful book, *Originals*, on becoming a trailblazer by choosing to go against the grain, battling conformity, and bucking outdated traditions, Grant discusses speaking truth to power and that when we climb up the moral ladder, it can be rather lonely at the top.

He writes, "Leaders and managers appreciate it when employees take the initiative to offer help, build networks, gather new knowledge, and seek feedback. But there's one form of initiative that gets personalized: speaking up with suggestions. In one study across manufacturing, service, retail, and nonprofit settings, the more frequently employees voiced ideas and concerns upward, the less likely they were to receive raises and promotions over a two-year period."

Grant goes on to define the "shaper" who speaks truth to power despite all odds: an independent thinker who is curious, non-conforming and rebellious in that they practice nonhierarchical honesty; and they act in the face of risk because their fear of succeeding exceeds their fear of failing.

John is not a city employee, and he has his own business, but the moral war depicted in Grant's description would come to life in John's experience as a councilmember pretty rapidly.

In 2020, John and I were busier than ever with his eye clinic practice. Our phone lines were inundated with calls for appointments daily. The clinic is John's semi-retire job after forty-two years of optometric practice. John wanted to provide eye care for the underserved population within our community. The clinic accepted almost all government insurance such as Medicaid and Medicare, which were rarely offered in the area. We believe in giving back to our community. At this stage of our lives, the reason is principle or legacy. Not just reward or profit. This is why the vice grip on our city with corrupt hands bothers us so much. Friends and family have given me credit over and over again for my grit, my persistence, and my support to John. This is not what I want. Give me resolution over credit any day. I'm not asking for copyright of a solution or recognition, as long as it does good in the world, particularly in our city.

It's my observation for forty-plus years that John had never been interested in politics or traditional community service, but when people literally come to our table at almost every restaurant in a ten-mile radius and beg John to run for city council, that they need him to prevent the city from going bankrupt, it's hard to shovel more food in our mouth and ignore the call! It's hard to wave to your neighbors from the porch, knowing they needed you to improve their lives, and you did nothing but share the same zip code.

Community is very important to us as a couple. With the first communities established 100,000 years ago, as Yuval Noah Harari notes in his international bestseller, *Sapiens: A Brief History of*

Humankind, we're far from the only ones who place so much value on it.

Harari writes, "Family and community seem to have more impact on our happiness than money and health. People with strong families who live in tight-knit and supportive communities are significantly happier than people whose families are dysfunctional and who have never found (or never sought) a community to be part of."

John's father, Perry, was an enthusiastic politician for many years, and he loved this community. There is a rocking chair sitting in our front porch that honors his many years as councilman of Demorest. Perry was a very wise man. He had distinctly said, "Mei, you're going to handle all the family business. John, keep practicing optometry, but you should *never* go into politics."

My son, Josh, and I tried to discourage John from running. Josh is a board-certified ophthalmologist in Dalton, Georgia, and an honoree of the Gold Humanism Honor Society, which recognizes achievements in humanistic patient care. In medical school, Josh went to Honduras with a volunteer group of medical doctors and tended to people in need. Needless to say, John and I handed down our altruism and sense of fairness to Josh. He also speaks up for what's right and fights for the underdog. We should have known John would not acquiesce since we all stood for the same things.

From his face full of sincerity, John said, "I love this town. I was born here. My father served the city for almost thirty years. I need to answer the call. And many people have been calling!" He chuckled nervously.

His words were the same for a few months leading up to the election, so it was time for me and Josh to stop asking, "Are you sure?"

I thought we would live happily ever after, drama-free, once we dissolved his eye practice in Cumming, which was an hour and a half's drive each way. With the city council position, we set up his optometry practice near home with the intent of going parttime. Earnestly, John thought he could handle the practice and he would have "spare time" to take care of the discontent of the local citizens through his shiny, new council seat. Not exactly.

In September 2019, soon after he became one of the candidates for the councilmen, John and I attended the monthly council meeting. It was during this event that the Demorest residents' discontent and anxieties were openly displayed.

During the public-comments portion of the meeting, Demorest resident Deborah Showalter speaking on behalf of the many residents stood at podium before a large crowd and read a letter requesting the mayor to resign.

The Demorest residents' concerns were about a civil lawsuit against Rick Austin, which accused him of fraud. The case was settled a week prior, and Rick and his company, Pegasus Drone Services, was ordered to pay plaintiff Kingwood Water and Sewer Services (KWSS) $60,000. Other concerns expressed in the letter below included City Attorney Joey Homans, who was not present at the meeting, serving as the mayor's personal lawyer throughout his civil lawsuit:

> "I have been asked to speak on behalf of the concern citizens of Demorest. I was chosen because I have a good rapport with you, mayor, and with city council. I stress I am not hostile here. I am not here to attack anyone but more as a protective mother tiger over her cubs and, therefore, please understand my position as a messenger."

> "Due to the recent case against you and your company...."

At this point, the mayor interjected, "I will not be discussing the settled case."

"The people have been justly informed by the press with the result that trust towards you has been breached. The people question how you can effectively continue as a public servant for our city with all trust gone further escalating the breach of trust is a conflict of interest exemplified by attorney Joey Homans, our city attorney, representing the mayor in matters that are not pertinent to our city in personal lawsuits. Questions of time divides become blurry as citizens want to know if work time for Mr. Homans is paid for by the city and has been used to discuss or conduct business regarding your lawsuits. To the people, this representation demonstrates a conflict of interest in separation of city and personal business. With this conflict, to serve one or the other, but not serve both, is a result of necessity.

"Another erosion of trust lays in the discovery that your business previously mentioned for the court case, Pegasus Drone is registered as a corporation in the State of Georgia and addressed in Demorest."

The mayor injected again, "Be cautious with your allegations." Deborah Showalter ignored the warning and continued:

"Pegasus Drone Services has never had a business license to operate in Demorest since 2014. This would potentially affect city water billing for a business, as well as city license fees. With this information, the people ask if your position as mayor a way to serve or circumvent city codes.

"An additional concern is with the settlement fees and court costs you are now responsible, the people want to ensure a strict accounting in all city funds and water funds be in place both for your protection and the protection of our city.

"As you have heard, there are many concerns by the citizens and, frankly, this is a brief summary. As spokesperson for the citizens, I am concerned for everybody.

"The overwhelming consensus of the community no longer believes you have the moral turpitude that represents a public servant entrusted to be the mayor of Demorest.

"With this understanding relayed to you, the citizens want to know if you feel you are still the best person to serve Demorest or are you the stronger person who can admit he is not?

"We respectfully ask that you consider resignation immediately for the protection and preservation of the city of Demorest."

As Deborah Showalter stepped away from the podium, letting her last words hang in the air, you could hear a pin drop in the audience. Rick Austin offered no response.

It is known that a business license is not required if one does not conduct business inside the city limit. However, the *Northeast Georgian* reported that the acting city manager Kim Simonds confirmed on the Thursday after the meeting that Rick Austin purchased a business license for the Pegasus Drone Services that morning.

In his response to the *Northeast Georgian* regarding the letter read by Deborah Showalter, the mayor dismissed all allegations and insisted, "The city is in the best financial situation that it has ever been in. We again, have more cash on hand, and building the reserve."

Actions by the public wrote a different love letter. When John campaigned for the position, we purchased twenty lawn signs and didn't use all of them. People threw money at us, wanting to donate, and we didn't take it. John felt that since so many people had urged him to run, they would come out and vote for him. August 2019 was the registry date for the vacancies as candidates. There were two vacancies and three candidates that qualified. He won with the highest vote.

John and I love this city. We work here and own properties here. Most importantly, John grew up here with many of the current residents and knows almost everyone in town. If it is home, we want it to remain livable. This place signifies loyalty and roots. We want to maintain the quality in our life. Conflict is constantly stirred up, but we should have peace.

We built a great deal of history here, but John rapidly learned this world of politics is like a country we've never been in. In his own words: "I base my life on right and wrong and doing what is right based on fact. Not in this world. Not in this environment. This is all character driven. And not the character inside someone's qualities; the character that laughs, explodes, wields power, shouts, cries for his way. Being in the middle of all this is a moral war zone."

John's father, Perry Hendrix, the mayor of Demorest, Georgia for four years, a councilman for twenty-eight years, and an executive at Johnson and Johnson. His mother, Betty, was a top sales agent for MetLife insurance Company, a former Sunday school teacher. Betty's father was a security guard at a local saddle tree factory. Both of John's parents were devoted Presbyterians and extremely intertwined in the community.

"Perry," as we know him as, was well-liked. During those days, Malcomb Honeycutt was the mayor, and the council was very peaceful. Years ago, one day during Thanksgiving, I was helping my mother-in-law prepare dinner and he breezed in and said, "I'll be back in fifteen minutes. We have a council meeting."

"Huh?" I said, mystified. "You're going to a council meeting, and it will only be fifteen minutes?" He assured me it would. I looked at my watch, stomach grumbling, and joked, "Okay, I'm hungry. I'm going to count your time!"

I started assembling the table. Low and behold, Perry popped into the kitchen fifteen minutes later! The council had voted for the topical stuff and cheerfully wished each other "happy holidays." Everyone was so friendly. This was the way to do city business.

Josh used to go with his grandfather to the old city hall and play around the counter entrance. These days, no one plays. The mayor will talk as if he is going to slit your throat if you say one wrong word. Our upstanding attorney, Abe, spoke up recently and the mayor barked, "You're not authorized to speak up!" Then he shot eyes of blue fire at the chief of police and ordered him to remove Abe. Chief Krockum wouldn't dare make a move because of Abe being a respected lawyer that could retaliate. This short incident scored press coverage, casting Abe in a negative light and brazenly reporting inaccuracies. The paper failed to report the most significant part; that the mayor tried to remove Abe from the meeting but could not.

Making Sense of a Changing Landscape

Parts of the county are referenced in my discussion of events because you can't help but compare locales in a county of 45,000 citizens. In essence, we Habersham County citizens share a lot of resources and budgetary concerns. Also, since this takes place in the South, fertile ground for storytelling, it's worth providing some local color as we go deeper into *Tricking the City*.

Resting in the foothills of the Appalachian Mountains, roughly ninety miles north of Atlanta, is Habersham County. Officially created in 1818 from the lands of the Cherokee Indians, Habersham County is named after Revolutionary War hero and U.S. Postmaster General Joseph Habersham.

Settlers came after the Indian Cessions of 1818 and 1819. They settled along the banks of the county's four major rivers:

the Chattahoochee, Soque, Tallulah and Tugaloo. The Northeast Georgia gold rush brought growth to the area, as the state was the largest gold producer in the country.

In 1838, the remaining Cherokee were removed via the "Trail of Tears."

Over 1,000 men of Habersham County bravely fought for the Confederate States of America, many losing their lives in the major battles fought in the eastern front of the Civil War. Between 1870 and 1900, Habersham County's economy flourished with the help of the railroads, the planting of fruits, and the founding of Piedmont University. Habersham County had a tourist attraction in Tallulah Gorge beginning in 1882. People would ride the rails through the Blue Ridge to see the "Niagara of the South."

The City of Clarkesville was charted and named for the Revolutionary War General and Governor John C. Clarke. When Clarkesville was incorporated and selected as the county seat in 1823, feuding over the selection with the city of Toccoa directly led to the formation of Stephens County in 1905 with Toccoa as its seat. Incorporated municipalities in Habersham County are Alto, Baldwin, Cornelia, Demorest, Mount Airy, and Tallulah Falls. At the high point or "Altus" of the railroads of the 1870s, the railroad line went through the area known today as Alto, which took their name from the railroad term. Baldwin was incorporated in 1896. It is named for Joseph A. Baldwin, who was an Atlanta-Charlotte Air Line Railroad official.

Demorest was incorporated in 1889 and was a *Temperance Community*. The City of Cornelia was built around 1870 in a grid pattern, forming the original city that can now be seen in the square blocks east and northeast of the central business district. On October 22, 1887, the city was incorporated as «Cornelia» in honor of the wife of the attorney who represented the railroad, Pope Barrow.

Depending on which way you're driving into Demorest, you may stumble on the Big Red Apple poised on the railway station grounds in Cornelia.

The replica of the north Georgia apple is seven feet in height and twenty-two feet in circumference. It weighs 5,200 pounds and is painted in natural colors. The apple is constructed of steel and concrete and was molded in Winchester, Virginia, in 1925. It was shipped to the town by train. It is erected on a concrete pedestal eight feet in height and six feet square at the base. The monument was donated by Southern Railway, and for many years a festival was held in celebration of the apples grown in the area.

At the close of the Civil War in 1865, the area where Cornelia is located was a typical mountain forest. The spot was so well-secluded that a moonshine still was operated without interference at the site of what is now the center of downtown. Cornelia was first a settlement around 1860. It was situated near the old boundary line between the Cherokee and Creek Indian tribes.

Habersham County has changed with the times while keeping its small community feel. Some examples of agricultural products from this county are poultry and apples. Fieldale Farms is a family business that has grown to become one of the largest independent poultry producers in the world. It is also Habersham County's largest employer. Other notable industries include the following: Ethicon, a Johnson & Johnson company, which develops innovative surgical products for laparoscopic and minimally invasive procedures; Mount Vernon Mills Inc., a diversified and integrated producer of yarns, fabrics, and finished products for the apparel, industrial, home furnishings, institutional and consumer goods markets; and Globaltech Industries, a candle manufacturer that has produced candles for companies such as Bath & Body Works, Curve, and Victoria's Secret.

In 2013, the estimated population was 43,300, which included 90.7% White, 4.0% African American, 1.1% Native American, 2.5% Asian, and 13.6% Hispanic. I have aided to the 2.5% population for about forty years.

Habersham is also the home of two institutions of higher learning: Piedmont University located in Demorest and North Georgia Technical College located in Clarkesville. As Piedmont University is practically a stone's throw from our house, I refer to it a lot in my story.

Habersham County residents are fortunate to have an award-winning medical facility to serve their health care needs. Located in Demorest, Habersham Medical Center is a fifty-three-bed not-for-profit acute care facility providing health care to more than 80,000 residents of Habersham and adjoining counties. Another important part of Habersham County lies two miles west of Cornelia. The Habersham County Airport boasts a 5,000-foot runway as well as a fuel station with 100 octane aviation fuel and jet fuel during regular business hours.

Here is what touches me about Habersham County as it relates to my life; it has survived Indian Wars, Civil Wars, and World Wars. It has survived droughts, boll weevils devastating the cotton industry and flowers, stock market crashes, and depressions. It will survive a corrupt consortium of local politicians hellbent on their own gain!

The start of Demorest is every bit fascinating as moonshine-soaked Cornelia. Demorest was founded in 1889 as a private endeavor of the Demorest Home, Mining & Improvement Company, named for William Jennings Demorest, an internationally known alcohol prohibition leader. William Jennings Demorest (aka W. Jennings Demorest) (1822–1895), from New York City, was an American magazine publisher, national prohibition leader, and, in collaboration with his second wife, Ellen Demorest, née Curtis, attained international success from his wife's development of paper patterns for sewing fashion apparel of the day. Together, they built a fashion manufacturing and merchandising empire from it. He and his wife launched five magazines and started a cosmetics company. He individually patented a sewing machine and a *velocipede* (or an early form of bicycle).

Demorest harbored lifelong political and religious aspirations. He is widely known for being a Prohibition activist and ran for mayor of New York City on the Prohibition ticket. He also organized the Anti-Nuisance League. In 1889, a group of people from Massachusetts, New Hampshire, Ohio, and Indiana moved to Georgia to establish a community that would have high moral standards. They decided that anyone who permitted drinking alcoholic beverages, gambling, or prostitution would forfeit their property.

When I was introduced to the city about forty-two years ago, Demorest contained 1,200 people. Everything is compacted downtown. Piedmont University was a small, private college that is prestigious. In fact, its prestige could, in part, be attributed to native Chinese Madame Chiang Kai-Shek, who, as "Soong Mei-ling," had enrolled in the college at the age of fourteen. Her father had sent all three of his daughters to the United States to be educated.

Decades later, after returning to Taiwan as the first lady, this same woman had founded my college in Taipei that I wasn't likely to have attended in the first place. It also didn't escape me that her middle name was "Mei." There is very little Asian history in these parts, so it's worth sharing that both of us Mei's developed our stories in Demorest, Georgia and Taipei, Taiwan. Absolutely uncanny!

Piedmont University also is central to the city workings of Demorest.

According to the *Athens Banner-Herald*, notable Piedmont

alumni also include Johnny Mize, who played baseball at Piedmont in the 1930s and went on to a Hall of Fame career in Major League Baseball, including five straight World Series crowns with the New York Yankees. Lillian Smith, author of the groundbreaking novel of interracial love, *Strange Fruit* (banned in Boston when it was published in 1944) also studied at Piedmont. Finally, emeritus professor the Rev. Dr. Barbara Brown Taylor, author of a dozen books on religion and spirituality and named by *Time* magazine one of the 100 most influential people in the nation.

I have always believed in being a steward of history and culture, playing my part in keeping it positive for the next generation. Demorest is worth it.

Chapter 3

INSPECTING THE SEWAGE

"Three things cannot be long hidden: the sun, the moon, and the truth."
—Buddha, Spiritual Teacher

DEMOREST MAY BE small, but it supplies water to all of Habersham County, which is a significant responsibility, not to mention a badge of authority. I wholeheartedly believe that Mayor Rick Austin sees a goldmine in this water well. It is intuition backed up by a tainted history of well-documented misdeeds, lawsuits, poisonous accusations, and public outcry.

I always give people the benefit of the doubt—heaven knows I expect the same, particularly these days when there is so much antitrust and hate-fueled attacks on Asian Americans.

But when the same themes ensue year after year, it may be contextually more than just someone's bone to pick. Rick's unbecoming reputation has created a messy swamp in Demorest though we're located in a part of the state nowhere near the coast.

Prior to setting his sights on municipal government, Rick served in the Georgia House of Representatives District 10 for two terms, 2009-2010 and 2011-2012, before he was defeated by John Wilkinson, who served for a decade until he was defeated in the banner political year of 2020. Rick did not rise on the state and national political ladder; he became county commissioner and then mayor. When Rick got elected, he let go of Dana Maine, the city attorney, who is now working for the insurance company and defending the city against a major lawsuit by Piedmont University. More on that soon. He pushed to replace Dana with Joey Homans, his right-hand man, and together, they have downgraded and degraded Demorest.

From his photography site chock full of clips from Trump rallies: "If you are a candidate or an elected official, you are either running or you are running behind." With that, I honestly wonder how he would assess himself as a leader, and as a mayor.

The Atlanta Journal-Constitution has deemed Demorest as a "politically and socially conservative community where 'repent' signs hang randomly along some of its busier streets and on a campus with long-standing ties to several religious organizations."

Are you starting to get a picture of the negative light on my city between scandals and scandalous intentions?

Arsenal of Accusations

The year of 2019, prior to John's election, was busy for Rick. He settled a lawsuit for $60,000 alleging fraud filed in Habersham County Superior Court. He had entered a contract to purchase a local water and sewer business (ironically!) in August 2017. The suit claimed that, after taking over collection of bills for the business, Austin funneled profits from the company, which were meant to pay operating expenses, to his own personal use in the form of auto parts for his car, a $10,000 cash withdrawal, and a computer from Best Buy. In turn, Kingwood Water and Sewer LLC, the lawsuit contended, could not pay bills owed to Georgia Power, Windstream and the City of Clayton. City Attorney Joey Homans represented Rick in this case.

Rick is also a professor of biology of twenty-two years at Piedmont University. He accused President James Mellichamp of sexual harassment in 2019 as a component of a lawsuit by another professor, Robert Wainberg, for wrongful termination after multiple accusations of sexual harassment by students. Rick cited an interaction with Mellichamp from 2012. That accusation was never brought up as a legal suit but has been cited in several motions, while Mellichamp and a board of thirty-six people have long called for Rick's resignation from the university given his position as mayor for seven years.

Regarding the sexual harassment he accused Mellichamp of, Rick made a statement to *The Atlanta Journal-Constitution (AJC)*: "I have always stood firmly for what is right and true," he wrote. "I do so now, not only for Dr. Wainberg, but for myself and all victims of sexual abuse, harassment, and assault. It is an abuse of power that happens to both men and women. I urge all victims to live courageously, speaking truth to power without fear of retaliation, free from shame and self-doubt. Only then can we shine light in those dark places where predators and perpetrators hide."

I can honestly say that I agree for a change with Rick's words here. However, I do not consider him to be a proponent of "speaking truth to power."

What's in the water?

All the sudden, the city has $6 million in revenue from the water fund. Revenue provided funding for a lot of services. The problem is that the citizens cannot understand wasteful spending on fancy equipment, or "toys," for the police department and the fire department, for example. Our police department has a budget of $850,000. With that amount of money, I can take that money and hire private bodyguards for every household! Throw in the fire department's budget of $600,000 in which the fire chief is constantly buying tools for himself. For comparison, Statham, a small town nearby, has a population of 2,700. Their police budget is $367,135 and they don't have a fire budget. They pay the same property tax that we do. To show you the degrees of separation between our two cities lately, Statham has earned Georgia Municipal Association's certification as a City of Ethics, which simply means that it adopted an ethics ordinance and resolution establishing five ethics principles for the conduct of its city's officials:

- Serve others, not ourselves
- Use resources with efficiency and economy
- Treat all people fairly
- Use the power of our position for the well-being of our constituents
- Create an environment of honesty, openness and integrity

In my mind, this is easy enough to aspire to, but some figures really have adifficult time living by these principles. Congratulations, Statham!

The majority of citizens here are senior citizens who don't have access to social media, to express their opinion. They read from the newspaper. Most have lived here for a long time if not for their whole life. They know John and the family. They often call or come straight to our door to inform him of something the mayor did instead of expressing their concerns by attending the council meeting. When they do, the mayor threatens or intimidates them in some way. He forces them to shut down the truth. It's a nonstop gag order! We all have an invisible red X taping our mouths shut despite all of our contributions.

The city's water provider started with only 600 customers and has grown ten times to 6,000. John's father's twenty-eight years of service for the city and Habersham County Water Authority definitely went toward this effort. A lot of citizens think the old pipes went into these towns to beef up infrastructure, so they're not sure what the water rate should even be.

I once read that someone asked why they have to pay for water in the first place. I thought this was an interesting question. EPA's explanation is that water utilities need to charge customers to build and maintain infrastructure—the water storage tanks, treatment plants, and underground pipes that deliver water to homes and businesses. The revenue is also used to pay the workers who provide you with water service day or night.

For the Love of Information and Instinct

One afternoon in January 2020, as I was learning of a new virus called "COVID-19" and its first cases in Wuhan, China, and hunting for more info, John came rushing through the door with the Moody's report summary on the city. Because of the expression on his face, I knew the information was pretty damning. John never exaggerated information or displayed theatrics. "We need to buy the full report, it's about the city's $10 million debt."

I went online and paid the $500 for a report to see for myself. (That was surely a cost the city will not reimburse.) Amazingly, it confirmed the $10 million debt tied to Demorest, breaking it down into line items, and specified two ratings: the water fund rating was BAA3, "stable," two ratings above a junk bond rating, but the city, much worse, one rating above a speculative junk bond rating.

The report listed possible factors that might improve the rating including:

- Service area growth coupled with improved socioeconomic factors
- Improved liquidity position
- Reduction in transfers to general fund

Just as individuals have their own credit report and rating issued by credit bureaus, bond issuers generally are evaluated by their own set of ratings agencies to assess their creditworthiness. There are three main ratings agencies that evaluate the creditworthiness of bonds: Moody's, Standard & Poor's, and Fitch. Their opinions of that creditworthiness—in other words, the issuer's financial ability to make interest payments and repay the loan in full at maturity—is what determines the bond's rating and also affects the yield the issuer must pay to entice investors. Lower-rated bonds generally offer higher yields to compensate investors for the additional risk.

Ratings agencies research the financial health of each bond issuer (including issuers of municipal bonds) and assign ratings to the bonds being offered. Each agency has a similar hierarchy to help investors assess that bond's credit quality compared to other bonds. Bonds with a rating of *BBB-* (on the Standard & Poor's and Fitch scale) or *Baa3* (on Moody's) or better are considered "investment-grade." Bonds with lower ratings are considered "speculative" and often referred to as "high-yield" or "junk" bonds.

How do we equate a "junk" rating with all this revenue?

If we were to drop one more rating, we wouldn't be able to get grants or funds for the city, which would be pathetic. Georgia has a good rating statewide. And we are home to Piedmont University. Does it want to be located in a city that is *bankrupt*?

Of course, it's one thing to talk about this highly sensitive and concerning matter over a celebratory dinner when conversation can be choppier than the chopped salad; it's another to come into a public forum as a fish out of water and present the facts. It took a great deal of courage for John to do this.

Unwanted Spotlight

City council meetings always start with a Christian prayer and recitation of "The Pledge of Allegiance." Sitting on one of the flimsy metal chairs in the audience, I observed the other members on the platform. The mayor sits in the middle. The city manager and city attorney are located close to the public space to the left at their own table, side by side. I noticed that the environment was already set up for debate and grievances. The room didn't have a positive vibe.

It was January 28, 2020. President Donald J. Trump's lawyers resumed his defense in the Senate impeachment trial on Monday, arguing that nothing he did amounted to abuse of power or obstruction of the House investigation into his actions regarding Ukraine. Auschwitz survivors marked the 75th anniversary of death camp's liberation. And the Supreme Court ruled in favor of the public charge rule restricting legal immigration. What I couldn't know is how the day would mark the next phase in our lives.

Even though the mayor doesn't vote on issues, it was clear who usually took charge of these meetings. He always wore suits, but his demeanor was one of rough rider, with a country edge, not a friendly mayoral figure that stood on the sidelines of parades and held babies for the cameras.

John revealed all the astounding information, framing the content as "financial transparency." He presented a handout concerning the bond rating for the City of Demorest. He noted that the Moody's (bond) rating for the City of Demorest dropped from *A3* to *Ba1*, in part, because of the transfers from the water fund to the general fund. This rating would prohibit the city from obtaining a loan if needed.

"Our water department has worked hard. It says on here it's strong, it makes money, it does a good job," John said passionately waving the report in his hand, "And what are we doing? We are crippling it!"

Joely Mixon, CPA, the city treasurer, who would also become a clever player tricking the city, commented, "Well, we've talked about reserves and the transfers coming over from water revenue, we talked about this every year when we do the budget. The only way to lessen the budget is to give up on the general fund side which is your public safety, your street services, and your administrative functions, etc., so that would be the way to reduce the transfer from the water revenue."

The city treasurer further reiterated, "The only way to reduce the number of transfers would be to curtail spending on services other than water or sewer."

Sitting in the last row, I smiled at John warmly and he had a twinkle in his eye when he said that he would donate his time and services to improving these grave mistakes for the city. He didn't just take over on the platform to deliver bad news. In true hero fashion, he also committed to repair the city's uneasy relationship with Piedmont College.

During the same meeting, John also mentioned that the acronym, *MEND* (Minimize Economic Negatives and maximize Development), might be the basis of a plan to turn the rating around. There were several comments from citizens and council members regarding this issue and the discussion continued as reactions in the room vied for attention.

While talking about cutting the budget on the general fund including police and fire, the mayor quickly injected, "Public safety was of primary importance," hinting his objection to the budget cut.

"No," a tall gentleman stood up from the audience and spoke loudly. I later learned that he was the president of the Piedmont University, Dr. James Mellichamp, "If you all were a family running your finances the way the city is running its finances, you'd be in the poor house. The children would've starved to death. We are fortunate to be in a healthy financial environment right now and the time to tighten your belt is during good times, not during bad times. I am sorry, but somebody here needs to take the bull by the horns and make some really tough decisions like these folks are talking about."

When the meeting was adjourned, as John was getting out of his seat to leave, the mayor turned to John and asked, "What was that all about?" as if John had instigated an attack.

"You lied to me!" John said. "You had a chance to tell the truth that night when I asked."

"Well, we were at the dinner…" the mayor sighed, trying to sound like a considerate friend.

"So, you chose to lie?" John said seriously while staring at him.

Rick spat with an evil look, "I don't give a shit!" then walked away.

The next day, John received the following email message from Dr. Mellichamp:

> "John, thanks for peeling back the layers of the onion last night. Folks need a big dose of reality and facts don't lie. Kristi Williams told me this morning that the mayor had directed her to suppress the information about the degradation of the bond ratings and to tell people who asked that they were being 're-scored.'
>
> Seems like that fact needs to see the light of day.
>
> All best, JFM"

Kristi Williams, formerly Kristi Shead, is associate vice president of finance/controller at Piedmont University. She was the former

Demorest city manager and is also the wife of Bert Williams, the managing director of Kingwood Water and Sewer, plaintiff of the case Kingwood vs. Pegasus and Rick Austin.

Two days after John's inaugural city council meeting, our local newspaper, *Northeast Georgia*, reported a response by the mayor which was absent when he was asked at the time of the meeting while the Moody's bond rating was being discussed. The mayor obviously allowed himself more time to prepared for a public comment. In the report, the mayor accused John's revelation on the city's financial issues as "inappropriate, misleading, and irresponsible." My assessment is that the truth hurts. Particularly when it was armed with evidence. Thus, negative adjectives were the only tools in this case for tricking the city.

The following week, in a Letter to the Editor titled "Exposing the Wizard of Demorest," Dr. Mellichamp wrote:

> "...New council member Dr. John Hendrix performed the role of "Toto". Just like the classic film version, the curtain was pulled back and the truth about the financial situation of the city revealed.

> "One needs only review a month or two of back issues from the Northeast Georgian to be overwhelmed with the platitudes emanating from Demorest City Hall to describe a fantasy world that exists only in the mind of one or two individuals.

> "The truth is that almost $10 million in bonds used by the city for improvements in the water system have been downgraded over the past four years to 'Junk Bond' status by Mood's. Why would Moody's do this? Because the city's operating budget has been running

an enormous deficit every year and the city has diverted revenue from the water department to make up for the difference. My question is who at the City Hall knew about the downgrading of the bonds, when did they know this, and what did they do about it?

"As president of one of the largest businesses in the city of Demorest and county of Habersham, I have more than a benign interest in these matters. Lastly, Piedmont College paid the city over $250,000 in fees for water and sewer service. Some folks may not agree with all the decisions we make at Piedmont College, but our balance sheets don't lie. If I ran the college the way city is running its business, my board would send me packing."

The reality is that between our friendly dinner and this meeting, more information about the mayor had come to light. Disturbing tales careened through the dark night.

The morning after the Moody's rating revelation, the new city manager, Kim Simonds, walked into John's office downtown. John asked me to join the meeting and take notes for him. In that, John's ear underwent surgery a few months ago and he was still encountering problem with hearing.

In John's exam room, Kim said: "The mayor had a reputation for walking into the office of City Hall and barking out instructions to the clerk or manager to give someone like a police officer or certain city hall employee a raise as much as an increase of $10 an hour. No justification. No documentation. He would ask for checks to be issued without proof or authorization of claims. There were accusations that he took the pool chemicals, which was purchased by the city for his personal use."

Kim went on to say that until the meeting last night, she was afraid to reveal Rick's abuse of power to anyone, as the mayor seemed to tightly control every aspect of the city operations either himself or by his "trusted" employees.

To disobey him, one might be looking for a new job instantly.

The mayor was also the highest paid mayor in the county, who gets paid twice as much as city council members when attending a meeting, $200. Councilmembers do not make a salary; they get paid $100 per meeting they attend.

The following week at the regular council meeting on February 4, 2020, when John and I walked into the municipal building, the room was packed, standing room only. Lawrence Bridges, who was sitting in the back of the room, got up and yielded his seat to me. I thanked him, then sat down.

The meeting started. Sensing the tension in the room, the mayor called for public decorum. "It is imperative that we operate with professionalism in the court." He was attempting to control the atmosphere in the room. "So, I ask that when people speak, they do so by not speaking over others and that we're polite and cordial. At the end of the day, we're all North Georgia residents; most of us are residents of the City of Demorest." This call, however, was soon breached.

Local resident, Deborah Showalter, was the first to speak during the public comments. She questioned the mayor about discrepancies in the city budget. "Mr. Mayor, your 2019 meeting fees were claimed with no explanation and several doubles, and even triple, meetings were called over a twenty-four-hour period. It's clear that it's become, by the record-keeping, a very regular habit that pay requests come via calls and emails," Deborah said. "Documentation is promised to be provided later; the check is picked up. The majority of the 2019 records provided by you, Mr. Mayor, do not match the requests for pay."

Deborah asked that changes to be made in the way meetings and payments were documented and that the council cap the number of meetings they hold at two per month. The mayor laughed, and arrogantly replied, "Thank you, ma'am."

John also spoke at the public comments, "There were comments made in the newspaper accusing me of being irresponsible and misleading for revealing the city's financial status. Presenting the fact, to me, is transparency. In my view, this is how our city should operate."

To this day, John has refused to take any money for his city council service. In contrast, Rick teaches at the college and has blatantly reported during his teaching time that he attended a meeting in order to get paid. A local organization sprang up and the president, in public comments, complained and requested an open record for these payments. The complainer, Deborah Showalter, is now a familiar name. She was punished for calling attention to this with eggs smashed against her house and a massacre of trash in her yard. She didn't give up. She approached John and provided evidence that Rick was abusing his power, strolling in the office, and asking the clerk to cut him a check, that he would provide documentation later. This activity had gone on for seven years, according to her. After John revealed the city's true financial status, the same complainer filled John in on other corruptions. Now we have more than one person to confirm the mayor's corrupted activities.

The mayor is empowered by his best friend, the city attorney, representing him in personal matters for twenty years. What I find in this new land we've been dropped into is, there is no right or wrong. You just ride into the Wild West and shoot your guns! This is our municipal government. A haven for the lawless.

A newly elected official, being the man that he is, John felt compelled to report these illegal activities. John spoke to the district attorney, who abruptly cut him off and snapped, "I will call you back." Note that the mayor supported this district attorney, who's yet to call!

Next, John made the drastic move of going to the FBI. Surreal, right? But you should know that the FBI has long waged a war against corruption in small towns across the country, reports *Washington Post*. In recent years, particularly throughout Texas, the feds have charged county officials involved in bid-rigging and kickback schemes, law enforcement officers who sold drugs they seized to other traffickers and even a state judge who took bribes for favorable rulings. The FBI's San Antonio Division launched twenty-three public corruption investigations in 2012, fifty-one in 2013 and sixty-four in 2014, authorities said.

In February 2016, in Crystal City, federal prosecutors alleged in early February that the majority of the councilmembers were engaged in a conspiracy to help one another take bribes from those wanting to do business with the government. One councilmember even had an illicit business of transporting illegal immigrants!

When John called the FBI seeking assistance, the investigator confirmed, "There's certainly crime involved here, but I won't get approval to investigate this because the funds it would take will be a far cry from the justice you will get."

John had exposed himself by attempting to do what's right and he had the doors slammed in his face.

Ever felt despair? This was the feeling. And so soon after occupying this council seat with the promise of good will.

As soon as John revealed the financial condition of the city openly to Demorest citizens and Rick didn't want to address the situation, John became enemy No. 1. And further down the road, the situation deteriorated. John will tell you, "Moody's prints facts. Here are the facts. I simply put the facts out there. I printed the report and distributed it in the meeting." Simple enough in context but quite tumultuous in consequences.

What Comes in the Light of Day

Wouldn't you know that all that fussing and fighting you see on the stage of city council is over a small percent of the whole budget, 18%, because 82% is already allocated legally? When the first bond rating was put out, it was good, but then with extra spending (like another $1 million tossed at the police department), our credit rating got knocked down.

Even with this flurry of unsavory knowledge, John wanted to keep his father's legacy alive through following in his footsteps while he had the opportunity. In fact, at a ceremony to honor John Popham's many years of serving on Demorest City Council at his last meeting attended as a councilman, Rick credited Perry Hendrix.

He stated, "Were it not for Malcolm Hunnicutt, were it not for Perry Hendrix, were it not for Grady Tench, were it not for John Popham, were it not for Paul Skelton, during those years when this water system was being built, and the hard work and the hard hours, folks we wouldn't have the services that we are able to provide to our citizens every day. We certainly wouldn't be able to roll the millage rate back six years in a row like we have. It was because not of what we're doing up here now, but because of what was done at that point in time—and that took vision, from the mayor, from the council to the city, to the city manager, to the people that implemented and built it and put it in the ground and took care of it, cultivating it like a garden."

Sadly, his touching words would be buried under a pile of duplicitous acts.

Chapter 4

ATTORNEY PRIVILEGES

"Courage is grace under pressure."
—ERNEST HEMINGWAY,
NOVELIST

A COUPLE OF days after John's tense debut on the council and rendezvous with Moody's, John and I, Nathan Davis and his fiancé, Tracie, attended a dinner with colleagues at the Piedmont University President James F. Mellichamp's home as newly elected city officials. He had quickly shown his support of John's problematic findings, which brought a certain level of comfort.

I found Dr. Mellichamp to be a stimulating, cultured, and kind man whose lifelong passions are education and music. You simply do not find this combination in a person every day. He even designed the Sewell Organ, which is housed in the chapel of Piedmont University, showcasing 3,691 pipes in the organ constructed of various metals and woods.

Dr. Mellichamp's forty-five-year performance career as an organist has spanned throughout the United States, Canada, Europe and Asia. His concerts include solo recitals at such notable venues as the Washington National Cathedral, Berlin Cathedral, the Notre Dame

Cathedral, and Westminster Abbey. It's no secret that his legacy is emblazoned in the university's newly reinvigorated Conservatory of Music to the tune of $10.1 million. It includes a new concert hall with adjustable acoustics, a grand foyer, acoustically isolated teaching studios, classrooms, student practice rooms, a digital music suite, music library/conference room, student/faculty lounges, and auxiliary spaces. Perhaps most extraordinary and headline-worthy is that the facility houses twenty-seven Steinway pianos. The handcrafted instruments, widely considered the finest in the world, are synonymous with prestige and quality. The pianos and Piedmont's designation as an All-Steinway School were made possible through a $1.5 million gift by an anonymous donor. This is truly a source of pride for a city of 2,000.

But we have figures like Rick and Joey killing the music.

They run the city like they own it. Joey, who is really what I call the "devil of this whole operation," was the city attorney since 2014, as soon as the mayor took office.

On paper, he was a dream in the field of law, as his bio professes: Began his career in 1986 in the public sector, serving as Assistant City Attorney for the City of Gainesville and then as Assistant District Attorney for the Northeastern Judicial Circuit. He joined Fox, Chandler, Homans, Hicks and McKinnon, LLP in 1989. He maintains a civil practice and has represented various public entities including Dawson County, City of Demorest, City of Lula, Hall County Board of Tax Assessors, and Etowah Water and Sewer Authority.

Unfortunately, Joey didn't use these credentials in the city's best interests. As first voiced by City Manager Kim Simonds in calling for his resignation in the spring of 2020, "since 2016, Demorest has paid him $317,000 to do no litigation, review items, talk to everyone who works for the city on the phone, mainly, the mayor, and attend city council meetings. Not a bad job for a parttime job. As an attorney that has been retained by the City of Demorest, he is legally obligated to work in the interests of the city."

We knew of Joey and his questionable alliance with the mayor long before these accounts.

Before John ran for this office, numerous people knocked on our door at all hours of the day or caught him in the yard, urging him to run for city council. They displayed their own vulnerability and pleas because John has a reputation of integrity and fairness, period. No games. *No tricks.*

One night, Nathan called and exasperated, said, "Did you see the writing on stop sign by your house? It says, 'get rid of Rick!'" The discontent is so obvious.

Rick Austin is a control freak. I'm sorry I have to use this kind of language, but I've also learned that these words are an understatement. The form of the city of Demorest is under the state of Georgia of assembly, council-manager format, which means the mayor is a ceremonial figure. The mayor does not vote unless there is a tie vote. City council makes decisions, and his description is to preside over meetings and sign any declaration of contract after approval and be a spokesperson for the city. Therefore, he has no authority according to the charter and cannot vote. City council is authorized to conduct business for the city overall. In the past, our city conducted business under the "strong-mayor" format and rubberstamped what he wanted.

Everything stems from this one charter; the charter of the City of Demorest, which spells out clearly what can and can't be done:

City of Demorest operates in the Council-Manager form of government, not a Mayor-Council (Strong-Mayor) government. In Georgia, cities may not change the form of government established in their charter without a local Act by the General Assembly. The power in this form of government is vested in the city council, not in the mayor. Similarly, the mayor has no administrative authority other than the duties outlined in Section 2.29(1)-(6) of the Charter.

With this as his guiding force, John has had to state more than once to the mayor: "As an elective official of the city, it is not my duty to obtain your permission for any inquiries made on the city's behalf, particularly when my assistance was requested by city employees and/or their families and the information was provided to me by the city manager."

But Rick has indeed, called the shots on many occasions. He appointed himself as interim city manager, which is illegal. He was authorizing purchases and billing the city for meetings he submitted. Because of the previous complaint last year, council members specifically requested the city manager to verify all meetings.

In April 2020 when the quarterly meeting claims were filed, the city manager called and informed John that the very first meeting verified on the mayor's claim, particularly with the Department of Transportation (DOT) could not be confirmed. The DOT reported that there wasn't a meeting. He stated in writing that he did not meet with Mayor Austin.

Serving the city in a meaningful way is more than attending meetings. It's about negotiating, networking, and allocating resources, and resolving challenges for residents. Talk about missing in action (MIA)! On top of it all, such actions usually accompany certain characteristics that I am yet to see.

For example, from this list of leader competencies cited in Mark Hannum's innovative book on purposeful leadership, *Become*, which was ironically published around the same time that John got elected, I cannot assign one to Mayor Rick Austin:

- Setting the vision, goal or direction
- Goal oriented
- Strategy and strategic thinking
- Financial acumen
- Resourcing the strategy with key people, investment, and time
- Process orientation
- Highly self-aware
- Highly self-regulating
- Curious
- Open
- Selfless
- Courageous
- Socially adept
- Adept working with group/team dynamics
- Collaborating with stakeholders

Let me give you an example of the absence of these competencies: On March 14, 2020, the state was ordered to go into COVID-19 lockdown. The outbreak of the coronavirus had now spread to all fifty states and brought with it a cloud of uncertainty and frankly, terror. Yet, city council continued with its business, which could be done virtually, just like most forms of business worldwide during this time.

When the conversations about integrating the city fire department with the county's fire service started, council members were open to negotiating an agreement with Habersham County. The city manager initiated a meeting with the Habersham County manager to explore the possibility of fire service conversion. John and Nathan were invited originally but Nathan did not attend due to a schedule conflict, so John and Kim met with the county manager, Phil Sutton. During the meeting, all agreed to first present an intergovernmental proposal in a "special called meeting" on March 31, 2020.

On March 14, 2020, Governor Kemp declared public health state of emergency due to COVID-19 and discouraged group gathering and encouraged social distancing. City Manager Kim Simonds encouraged everyone to attend via Zoom or Facebook Live. Joey, the city attorney, insisted on attending in person since this had to do with a fire services intergovernmental agreement despite the fact that neighboring Hall County, where Joey lived, had just confirmed twenty-two cases of coronavirus.

As soon as John aligned with Kim, urging that the council attend virtually, Rick immediately sounded off the term "back-door meeting" and other unbelievable statements in the following e-mail:

> "I respectfully disagree." The mayor wrote in his email response, "Appropriate training of the newly-elect would have solved many of the self-inflicted problems we now face as a city. Closed door meetings and back-room politics that purposefully leave out the mayor and other members of Council is shady. We did away with good-ole boy politics in this city some time ago. We are going to operate in the light of day. Excluding our attorney, not to mention many in the public that are clamoring to have an opportunity to hear and be heard on the subject of eliminating out fire department, reducing the fire coverage of our city, giving away our trucks, equipment, and buildings, and increasing taxes by allowing the county to potentially implement a Special Fire District is just wrong. I wanted to hold this important subject off until which time the public could actively participate. The fact that the two newly elected officials are pushing so hard to have this meeting on this subject, despite the

Declaration of a State of Emergency by our Governor, leads me to no other conclusion that you want this discussion to occur without a fully involved constituency. Shame on you."

"Really, Mr. Mayor?" John mumbled, "What about those meetings you attended without notifying the council and charged the city $200 per meeting? The shame is on you as you are tricking the city once more."

Once John cited section 3.12 of the City Ordinance, stipulating that the city attorney attend the meetings only as directed, and reminding Rick that in February 2020, the city council voted to authorize the city manager as the point of contact to initiate any required legal services before any legal fees can be paid. In essence, Joey could attend the meeting at his own choice, but the city would bear no financial responsibility for his travel expense.

Rick doesn't play nice with rules and regulations. He responded with authoritative charm: "We need Joey in the room Tuesday evening for a number of reasons. For those of you concerned about fees, he's going to get paid whether he is on video or in person. Please plan on attending, Joey. Those that are worried about contracting the disease should utilize the audio/video options that are available. In other words, this is America and Joey, as a valuable, professional employee of the city, can make the determination himself."

Then he had the audacity to put in an invoice for attending that meeting! The council withdrew this meeting, claiming the threat of COVID-19. Rick had shut it down. Still, the words made it to the public, which infuriated residents, as it screamed the possibility of more corruption—even though good guy John was at the helm and there would be no improper behavior or decisions.

Protestors came out in all their maskless and reckless glory. As expected, the county commissioners were pressured from the mayor's trolls, students, and mostly non-Demorest residents, thus had to cancel the presentation on the Fire Conversion proposal. Rumor has it that the mayor used this tactic of cajoling students to just show up during his reelection in 2017 by offering good grades for the students' votes. This upset a lot of parents. When the students registered to vote here, the parents outside the city of Demorest could not claim them on the tax return, He won the reelection by eight votes.

Crooked Media

If you read the local press of *Northeast Georgian* and *Now Habersham*, you will instantly see those reporters around here side with the mayor and city attorney like a seesaw that never tilts back down. The mayor is always allowed to rebut what the council members say and twist it to his favor. The one of two newspaper district editors is the son of the editor of *Northeast Georgian* and ultra-conservative. Nothing they say will side with liberal leanings. Biased or not, do know that the newspaper content is all considered "premium content" online—it's like trying to get into a fortress to read a basic article!

When *Now Habersham* echoed Rick's lies that the council was trying to simply get rid of our fire department, which makes no sense obviously, and excluding the mayor from discussions, Nathan wrote a scathing opinion piece, stating, in part:

> "Habersham County offered us an opportunity to allow a fire presence in our city utilizing their personnel and equipment at the same location the current FD is located. Current firefighters would not be thrown to the "wolves" but would be employed by the county if they so choose. As for figures, try this on for size, the county will charge Demorest $130,000 per year for fire

service (for identical service)—the Demorest budget is approximately $650,000. Surely, you can do simple math. Doesn't take rocket science to figure it out. These funds will be used to pay down our debt and possibly lower property taxes in the future. Leading readers to believe that Demorest would be "giving away" the building and the equipment to the county is a total falsehood. The current FD equipment would be put out to bid and sold (with the proceeds used to pay down our serious debt). The current FD building would be used to house county EMS and the FD and would be rented to the county at a fair marketable price. The ISO rating would not be affected, nor would it affect any of our insurance premiums.

"Demorest residents should be thrilled to have the EMS so close to our city as the response time would be minimal. Our city is home to many senior citizens and most of them will call upon EMS at some time or another. Yes, there are strong opinions and feelings based upon the rumor mill and we are sorry that you chose to fuel the rumor mill with the misinformation you shared. You are no friend to Demorest."

Two months into his council position and being a rather quiet guy in person, I was surprised that Nathan took it upon himself to respond to the press and in such a "Mei" way, I confess. I believe in a no-nonsense way of communicating when it comes to serious matters. It's a family trait. I was thought to be open-minded and always encouraged something new, including a new or unpopular view. My family is pretty expressive, by Asian standards at least. John was also my mother's heart. Every time his name was mentioned, she would literally put her hand on her heart. I can't imagine how she would respond to any kind of ill treatment of him.

I have a collector's edition of emails that Rick has written to council members. You will rarely find a compliment, or complimentary words, for that matter. Some are downright nasty, either barking orders or chastising someone for not taking an order.

I still think of Perry's words: "Do not let John get involved in the city's politics!" He could never know the real reason that he shouldn't have gotten involved: a mayor obsessed with self-gain and local dominion.

Our son, Josh, and I urged, "Are you sure this is what you want? When you get into that position, we can't do anything for you. You will be standing in the spotlight." Approximately a year and a half later, John will still tell you that he thought this council seat would just be numbers. He has served on state boards before. He was the president of Optometric Association in which all 700 members or so acted professionally. They had a budget. They went head-to-head on issues as optometrists, but their discussions were always civil, always dignified. This is what John expected even more easily from city council because there would be no industry interests or dare, I say, egos.

When Piedmont University President Mellichamp compared Demorest politics to "Wizard of Oz" in an open letter to the press, John's water and sewer bond comments were strewn together with Piedmont University's water bill of $175,000. These are the headlines of the day! Piedmont University's "failed attempt to pay city water bill of $16,971.82, wrote Mellichamp "was processed for payment by us to our third-party payment system, Paymerang, on February 20th, but they failed to get the payment to the city on that date. "In speaking with Paymerang today, my staff found out that they called the city and attempted to pay the account but someone at the city denied the payment stating that we had to pay the account in full plus the late fees before any payment would be accepted. When I contacted the city to find out if it was true that they would actually deny a $16k+ payment while the late fees are being disputed with Paymerang, I was told that the mayor was at the counter at the time when the payment attempt was made and that he denied the payment."

This begs the question, why would the mayor act in this manner against not only his own employer, Piedmont University, but also the city he represents, Demorest? Isn't refusing a $16,000 water payment hurtful to the city's business? Is this the behavior of a mayor? In reality though, this behavior and overblown command of control is consistent with how he treats city council—without legitimate power.

Chapter 5

TALKING TRASH

"Bad company corrupts good character."

—Menander,
Dramatist

If I could read a toxicity meter for the city (similar to the stethoscope example in my introduction), it may take my breath away. But as I am reminded in Tricia Brouk's timely book, *The Influential Voice*, nothing can take my voice away.

"Powerful and influential voices need to be heard so they can encourage and facilitate understanding, compassion, and love while igniting and inspiring the change we need so desperately as a society. Remember that speaking your mind may encourage someone else with poignant knowledge and experience to do so also. If everyone holds back, what will happen? Silence is considered to be violence—or at a minimum, approval of the situation—at times like this."

I consider my story, *Tricking the City*, my assignment for sharing my influential voice. I know some voices will object to what I have to say, but maybe some voices will be empowered.

When a citizen complains to John as an elected official, it is his duty to take some kind of action and reassure the citizen. I mentioned that he had even gone to the FBI, who gave him a lot of time and consideration to finally affirm there was a crime: theft. He suggested we go to GBI (Georgia Bureau of Investigation). By this time, Rick had already wrangled protesters over our police chief being fired (then quickly reinstated). That was in April 2020, a few weeks before Black Lives Matter assembled all over the world. Had the following incident in Demorest happened in June of 2020, Rick wouldn't have stood a chance to create the mayhem he did.

George Cason, a police officer, had posted negative comments about the city for purchasing "nice trash cans" and created a Facebook rhapsody. He posted, "When did the citizens of Demorest vote on getting new trash cans? Guess we better start watching our water bills and start looking for the maintenance fee that will most likely be tacked on to it to reimburse the $7,000 they spent on those trash cans."

When the city manager, Kim Simonds, sent the screenshot to John, he was flabbergasted. "Nonsense! The council voted to provide the trash cans to the residents free of charge," John exclaimed.

You know by now we are very loyal people. John urged Kim to find out if there were any "official" rules against posting these negative comments about your own city employer.

Kim approached John and Nathan, to back her up in reprimanding the officer. Then she wrote to Robin Krockum, our police chief, urging him to fill out a disciplinary form on George's misconduct, attaching screenshots of the comments made by George on Facebook and the section in our employee handbook that refers to this type of infraction.

Well, the police chief's response same day after looking into the issue was quite studious. He advocated that the comments were made from his personal Facebook page while he was off duty. George never identified himself as a city employee or acted in his official capacity as a Demorest police officer. He pointed out that the courts have ruled on these issues in the past—such as Pickering v. Board of Education, covering public-sector employees and their First Amendment rights (*1968*...intentionally emphasizing the year of 1968)—and more current laws include social media posts such as Facebook.

Robin also noted Garcetti v. Ceballos (2006), covering on-duty and off-duty speech by government employees. The court ruled "When public employees make statements pursuant to their official duties, they are not speaking as citizens for First Amendment purposes, and the Constitution does not insulate their communications from employer discipline."

In the end, Robin refused to write up George, citing that "as a leader, he strived to balance protecting the interests of the city, as well as protecting the rights of my officers while maintaining high standards and expecting the very best from them.'

Kim was livid.

His answer did not satisfy her because she discovered that George had actually posted the comments on the public forum, Voice of Habersham, and his profile identified him as a Demorest police officer. Furthermore, the statement he posted was against his very own employer, City of Demorest.

Kim vowed to "stew" on her response overnight. We didn't know what her stewing would bring. Could she have let this infraction go if the police chief himself, our department head, did not behave in this questionable manner?

Police Chief Robin Krockum's credibility spoke for itself, and we have been fortunate to have him. He has received 3,945 hours of training during his law enforcement career. At the time of his appointment, Krockum served as patrol commander/training officer/grants manager for the Habersham County Sheriff's Office, supervising twenty-six deputies within the patrol division, K-9 unit, school resource, SWAT, and the traffic unit. He joined the sheriff's office in 2009.

Prior to that, he served as chief of police in Alto, Georgia (p. 1,172) at a department he established. Krockum served as assistant chief of police in Demorest from 1996-2006. He also has been a 9-1-1 dispatcher and a security officer.

With these impeccable credentials and representation of Demorest, was his behavior commiserate? That was the question. No, according to Kim, the chief also consulted the city attorney without notifying her, so she lashed out that he was being disobedient. She fired the police chief without thinking carefully. A warning would have been acceptable. But yes, as a city manager, she has authority to terminate an employee when necessary.

"I know Kim has the authority to terminate, but I do not want to see the chief terminated, at least, not because of this," John said to me as he paced around my desk. "I think a termination in this case will be too harsh and unjustified."

John urged, "Kim, you ought to think if this is the last resort. If you fire the chief now, you will face harsh criticism." Kim assured John that she would go down to the police department and talk to the chief and give him another chance.

John hung up the phone and said, "Hopefully they will work something out."

Within an hour, John's cell phone was ringing. Sitting at my desk, I could hear Kim on the speaker with a passionate diatribe. All I heard from John: "You *what?*" I knew it wasn't good news. Kim explained to John that she went to the police department hoping to talk to the chief. Surprisingly, Rick Austin was there, shouting at Kim, "You had no right to say anything to the chief."

She informed John in the most quintessential Southern twang, "I told Rick that I have *every right* and *authority*."

According to Kim, Rick called the city attorney, roaring, "Joey, she cannot fire the police chief, can she?"

Sighing, Joey confirmed, "I'm afraid she can." And then the words came after she had stewed enough: "You're fired," Kim stated with every right and authority to the chief.

Right after the phone call from Kim, Nathan called John with excitement, "Kim fired him!"

"I know…" John barely released the words from his mouth.

Worrying for John, I couldn't help but speak loudly into the speaker, "Nathan, try not to be too excited right now. You all need to brace yourself as all hell is going to break loose."

Within an hour, we learned that Rick called the owner of *Now Habersham*, Joy Parcell, and she immediately paraded to the station with a camera crew and interviewed Rick, same day.

On April 17, 2020, Rick Austin's Facebook feed read:

> The citizens of Demorest should be outraged at the termination of Chief Robin Krockum. He has led our city to the number one police department in the state for the past three years in a row…a feat never accomplished before. He implemented vacation checks on homes. He implemented elder care to check on our elderly citizens. As a certified instructor, he has trained not only our officers, but others throughout our county. Chief Krockum stood by his officer's 1st Amendment Right to free speech and backed it up with court cases involving government employee speech…and he did so with polite professionalism. Citizens should know that neither me nor Councilman Moore were consulted or informed that

this was being considered. Citizens should also know that no official communication from manager Simonds has been sent to Mayor and complete Council. There is no room in our city for back-room politics, back-room swearing-ins and shady deals. Those days should be gone. Make no mistake, the city took an enormous hit today and we are less safe as a community. The concerted effort by the two newly elected councilmen and the city manager to dismantle public safety in our town has begun...and everyone should be concerned. Make your voice known. Call city hall and tell the manager and Councilman Davis and Councilman Hendrix how you feel. Robin Krockum is one of the finest men I know. He and his family deserve better. Our police department employees deserve better. I humbly ask the community that he has served so diligently to support him and stand with him as he has done for us countless times. #keepkrockum #supportpublicsafety

This was only the first scathing note that Rick wrote against city council. In no time, a huge gathering took place. In the early morning of the scheduled council meeting, John received a call from Kim. "A platform was assembled right in the front of the municipal building with microphones and speakers. I called the company that build the platform and the owner told me it was the mayor who ordered the platform," Kim said, with uneven breath. "No permit requested or issued by the city for this platform." Not even any consultation with the city manager to start operating this public circus. Rick's followers, who were mostly non-residents of the city, had planned to block the door to the municipal building. The platform was deemed illegal without a permit and thus, was taken down on the same day before the meeting. When he was asked for comments by news media after the dismantling, Rick said, "Don't tell my wife I paid for that platform!" This is the mayor who supposedly represents our city.

When asked why he was so passionate about going against the city manager, Rick tried to be a lawyer, rambling in his authoritative voice that it was his constitutional right to go against the city manager. Naturally, Rick had refused to write up the police chief for his behavior, but he quickly went online to chastise Kim, which stirred up mass negativity in the form of comments:

> "Kim Simonds about to find out just how much authority she doesn't have. Firing a great Police Chief and an even better man, because he refused to violate someone's rights. Later Tater. Welcome to McDonald's, my name is Kim, how may I serve you."

> "So tired of outsiders pushing the good ones we have in the forces away just because they can agree. It was in poor taste and for her to take all matters in her own hands was terribly wrong. Robin is an upstanding officer, leader and regular folk that would give you the shirt off his back. She needs to go. And who she appointed as interim was a very poor choice, maybe she should've dug into why he was replaced to begin with."

> "I was born there; raised there and want to see my small hometown continue to be successful."

> "I served in the U.S. Marine Corps & under the U.C.M.J. a service Person Does NOT have the Right of Free Speech WHILE Serving BUT Police Officers don't serve

under the U.C.M.J.! They have All the same Rights as any other Citizen but sure can't tell it by this Bitch's actions!"

"Demorest and Baldwin are the most corrupt cities in Habersham, and I AM SICK of city council thinking they are the only citizens who matter. Chief is a good man who stood up for his employees, and the city didn't like it. that just proves the city is nasty."

One year later, Kim is still attached to this scandal and the reputational damage of her rash, highly publicized decision.

After learning about the firing of the police chief, John was trying to reach councilman Sean Moore all afternoon without result. Nathan recommended Krockum's predecessor Greg Ellingson, who was removed and transferred to the public work department three years earlier, as the interim police chief. John was informed by Nathan that Kim was able to arrange a probate justice to swear in the interim chief in the same evening to ensure public safety.

As I recall, Nathan and Kim were at the swearing-in ceremony. Nathan called John afterwards and invited John to join him, Tracie, and Greg for a glass of champaign to celebrate Greg's new position as the Demorest interim police chief. John declined, citing COVID-19 lockdown, but he wanted to hear from councilman Sean Moore before taking one step further. I think he had already sensed the imminent political storm.

Sean Moore finally returned John's call and informed John that he would be attending the special called meeting on April 28, 2020, to vote on Ellingson as interim police chief. "Sean is fine with Ellingson as the interim for now," John told me, "But I am still uncomfortable with Chief Krockum's termination...a reprimand would have sufficed."

Soon after that, Kim had to retain an attorney from the Denton

Law Firm to handle these troublesome issues since the city attorney was uncooperative, using the conflict of interest as an excuse.

On April 28, 2020, John was attending the meeting telephonically from home. The meeting was quickly blocked from happening by Rick, who was standing outside the municipal building with a group of protesters and refusing to attend the meeting. According to Kim, Sean Moore and Nathan Davis arrived at the municipal courtroom, then Joey Homans, who was standing outside with the protesters too, entered the building and whispered something to Sean in his ear.

Sean then gathered his folders while saying, "I am uncomfortable attending this meeting." He left with Joey. Kim said that she had no choice but to call off the meeting due to lack of quorum.

A week later at the regular council meeting, Kim tried again. This time, a microphone was set up so citizens could be heard. Outside during a roaring thunderstorm, more than seventy-five people—unmasked and unhinged despite Georgia's ongoing state of emergency due to the coronavirus—gathered to watch a live feed of the council in action on a big-screen TV. And so, the people spoke; the council listened. They did an about-face, voting unanimously to reinstate former Police Chief Robin Krockum. The running joke is that he was sworn in for a *third* time: initially, in the special council session, and on TV.

Protestors had camped out with pizza waiting for the chief to be rehired. I saw them as Rick's fan club. Most of us did.

Two hours before a Fox5 report aired, Kim wrote to reporter Dale Russell to say: "There was NO closed-door meeting last night. The special called meeting was canceled due to a lack of quorum. I should not and cannot comment on personnel issues. I can, however, say that Chief Krockum WAS NOT terminated for his refusal to discipline his officer. Our mayor has meticulously cultivated a culture of organizational dysfunction that has rendered some city departments unmanageable. We are working hard to correct that and unfortunately in that process, hard decisions must be made."

John and I believe in loyalty, personal or professional. John said to me, "I do not agree with Kim for her decision to fire the chief, but I know that she has the city's best interest in heart. For this reason, I am compelled to help her weather this storm and hopefully will shield our city from any further social and political turmoil." I agreed and offered my support.

I admit, one hard decision in the midst of this debacle was to remain friendly with Nathan, as he literally threw John under a double-decker bus while all of this was going on. On Saturday, April 18, 2020, Nathan Davis contacted John in the evening. I could hear him on the cell phone speaker, "I have been talking to an attorney about the Sunshine Laws and the legitimacy of the interim police appointment. I couldn't comprehend all the legal terms. Maybe you or Mei can talk to him," Nathan said, knowing John had not been comfortable about the police chief situation.

In my view, this step should have been taken before any decision was made. But given the lack of confidence in the current city attorney, John agreed to call Erik Kennedy, the attorney. During the first telephone discussion, John and I were not very impressed with the legal research and the solutions offered by Kennedy. Kennedy then suggested John and Nathan to contact another attorney, Kushner, who was supposedly an "expert" in the Georgia Sunshine Laws. Nathan and John spent thirty minutes discussing the Krockum and Ellingson case with Kushner and he assured them that no Sunshine Law was broken. The consultation cost $650 and John end up paying for it.

One week later, Nathan forwarded John an invoice, which he

received in the email from Erik Kennedy on John's account in the amount of $4,800. Charges dated back to April 3, which was way before John's initial contact with Kennedy. The bill indicated that the pre-April 18 charges were all incurred by Nathan. I called Nathan and told him that I would contact Kennedy's office to request a revision of the charges since we should not be billed for charges incurred by him. Nathan quickly excused himself from the phone conversation and would not return any calls thereafter for at least six months. Then out of nowhere, we received a shock-and-awe email message loaded with contrived formalities on May 1, 2020:

"Councilman Hendrix,

Please excuse my delay in responding to your emails. After consulting with my private counsel, I have determined that these communications, the various phone conferences and various meetings fall outside the parameters of what we are permitted as elected officials and violate the open meetings requirements of the Georgia 'Open and Public Meetings Act' commonly referred to as the Georgia Sunshine Laws. Accordingly, I will no longer be communicating with you in any improper manner going forward.

"Further, under the Act, due to the requirement that our meetings be open and public, I feel that it is necessary to disclose this information to the people of Demorest. Accordingly, I have put together the enclosed press release outlining my involvement.

Respectfully,

Nathan Davis"

On that same day, his formal press release appeared in *Now Habersham* before his email reached John, admitting wrongdoing in the form of "unauthorized meetings" and phone calls with me, John and Kim about an attempt to hire another police chief. It didn't work and then it turned into a dog and pony show. The paper published Nathan's press release verbatim and it implicated John in several instances. The fact was that John and I were both in COVID-19 locked down at home since March 18, 2020. Neither of us had gone anywhere for months. Nathan's act was deceiving, baseless, and unforgiving. Not only did he place a target on John; Nathan also put a target on his own back.

After Nathan's press release, John was inundated with calls from Demorest residents for several days. Thankfully, many calls were supportive of John and expressed their trust in his innocence. Most of them were very upset for what Nathan had done. In fact, one email from a local citizen accurately described his unusual demeanor:

> "I have known Nathan Davis for 12+ years. My family and I supported him when he put in his bid to run for one of the vacant City of *Demorest, City Council seats* in addition to offering financial help with his campaign signs he requested clerical assistance from me, on several occasions in the past, for which I complied.
>
> "We were willing to help since the government in Demorest is in dire need of new ideas and clarity.
>
> "It was discovered that Councilman Davis has difficulty translating his thoughts and ideas into a cohesive written statement. Councilman Davis shared with me that he had issues in school with writing and reading difficulties, it led me to believe that he may suffer from dyslexia,

and I wanted to help him. Before he was elected, he would share his thoughts and ask me to incorporate those thoughts and ideas into a cohesive written statement. His goal was ultimately to run for Mayor when the current Mayor's term expired. He believed if he got his 'foot in the door' as a Councilman the citizens would see that he would make a good Mayor and when the opportunity arose, he would throw his 'hat in the ring.' He named Mrs. Hendrix, wife of Councilman John Hendrix, in his 'statement.' John Hendrix was elected to the other vacant City Council seat and is married to a very talented woman, who Councilman David stated to me that she was one of the smartest women he knew. He also told me that she could help him with his writing. He then ceased asking for my help and the assumption was that Mrs. Hendrix was assisting him.

"After reading his so called 'confession' to the press, it is with great concern that I have to ask if I will be held liable for my role in helping someone who obviously has a reading/writing handicap? At no time did I edit the content relative his thoughts and intentions and what he wished to convey to the recipient of the emails."

The mayor may be stimulated by the attention and popularity plays on the chessboard between media, citizens and council, but John is not accustomed to this. John is not this person. He is simply an advocate for sensible spending. An innocent in all else. As such, he was horrified to see Nathan's public announcement naming him in a series of shocking city council crimes, with his moral compass on display.

Everyone claims they are close to John. Everyone knows where

"Dr. Hendrix" lives. The house of integrity. In light of the firestorm against Kim, John paid $3,000 toward her attorney. He was going to quietly pay for it to help with the burden, but it was speculated that Piedmont University gave her this money.

John had an appointment with his cardiologist in the afternoon of the council meeting. John was not planning on attending the meeting knowing that we would not be back in time.

On our way home from Atlanta about ten minutes from home, I had felt the urge to urinate. "I am glad we are almost home. My bladder is complaining," I said to John. Then a call came in from Kim. "We are in the executive session and Rick is threatening to have my job tonight if I don't tell him who help paying for the attorney fee." John turned to me, "Will you be okay if I take care of this first?" I nodded. "I will be there in five," he said to Kim like Superman on a mission.

John was so furious and eager, he kept driving. Once we skidded into the meeting spot, John left the engine running because it was blazing hot in August, and he took the key...but left his phone in the car. I was holding my water for forty or so minutes! One of the ladies from the local citizen action committee called me to get the latest scoop, and I explained my predicament to her.

She gasped, "Oh my god, I feel for you, Mei! Why can't you use the bathroom there?" She was coming from a place of common sense, but I didn't want to disrupt the meeting. I think I was afraid of what I would see and hear, too, during their executive session.

Suddenly, with the engine still going, I realized that I could drive the car home then get my own car key! I took off up the steep hill from the parking lot and raced home. Our red Jaguar F-Pace must have looked like a spinning UFO. When I returned to the meeting to pick up John, he was in a fever over what had just taken place. Faces in the parking lot were flustered, including Kim's.

I hoped that Kim was grateful for John's actions to save her from getting fired. What's awkward about her legislative power is that everyone knows she lives in Clayton, not Demorest. She tries to make herself look good from all sides. She has the power to speak up, but she doesn't want to face the mayor's criticism. The hostility between them is as thick as a muddy swamp, but Kim was working in health care before Rick coaxed her into running for city manager. At one time at least, he had thought enough of her to recruit her for the job and all clerical duties for the city.

After she fired the police chief, threatening his very system of power and brand of nepotism, Rick even went so far as having the city's IT personnel break into Kim's email account while she was on vacation. I had personally urged her to secure any files before she left town. Sixth sense! The first thing she did when she came back from vacation was call John, bellowing, "You wouldn't believe what happened!"

Rick had persuaded the IT guy there was an open-record request, so he needed to retrieve this information. Once he called openly at the council meeting for her to be fired. Sean Moore motioned to terminate her, but no one seconded it, so the motion to fire her had failed. He tried every medium to terminate her.

These local events were transpiring while leadership, in all faces and phases on the international stage, squirmed under a microscope in the press around the clock. Full disclosure, we have TV news going throughout our day. CNN's world headquarters is in Atlanta, so we may be a little influenced by that source of pride. From somewhere in the house, I heard that three-term New York Governor Andrew Cuomo had a 71 percent approval rating due to his daily pandemic response actions. I thought, his job is so utterly challenging, but he showed great courage, compassion and transparency. We deserved this kind of leadership in Demorest.

People should know John and I are not involved in community service for money or politics. I have told John that if he runs again, I will divorce him! People love my advice, solutions, and troubleshooting, but some do not like my background or my appearance. I don't look like them. Because of my Asian face, they want to defer ultimately to John.

Once I wrote a speech for John and a department head came up to him after with a toothy smile. He said, "Dr. Hendrix, I know you didn't write that speech. Your brilliant wife did." I flat-out walked away the moment he made that comment.

I told John years ago, "You don't have to state who's doing what. I don't want to be in the spotlight. I'm happy being the busy bee behind the scenes."

With his appointment on city council, there is not much room to help behind the scenes though. I can't make phone calls on his behalf or write oratory for him to deliver. I had emphasized, "You better be ready to be in the public eye." He had thought he was helping, that everyone was his friend. Before conflict, before slanted local media, most *were* friends.

When the big Moody's announcement occurred, reporters chased him down for comments. This type of attention has been nearly a daily affair. The best service I can offer John and the City of Demorest is to describe all within these humble pages, truly.

I will boldly state, in my own influential voice, I fear there is a conspiracy to make the city go under; if the city is downgraded and no longer able to pay its debt, another city or county, even a private equity firm can come in, pay the $10 million debt, and capitalize on $37 million in assets that our water holds. People don't realize that, but the council members have confirmed this possibility.

Chapter 6

LITTLE TOWN FULL OF DRAMA

"Gossip is the opiate of the oppressed."
—ERICA JONG,
SATIRIST AND POET

I AM GOING to share a guilty pleasure with you: *Demorest City*, a tongue-and-cheek blog that gave me a chuckle every time I checked for posts during this crazy year. The content provider, "Belshazzar," shared a post titled "Cookies!" featuring the mayor with the character, Cookie Monster, from the popular children's TV show, "Sesame Street." The blurb was: "If you can't find Mayor Rick Austin, all you have to do is looking for piles of money. The next pile of money that Mayor Austin is going to have input on how it is spent comes in the take from the Special Local Option Sales Tax. Each of Habersham County municipalities are given a piece of the money. Demorest is getting $1.7 million and what does Mayor Rick Austin want to do with the money. One thing is for sure, Mayor Rick Austin will vote for something that is primarily good for Rick Austin."

I've been asked if I know who Belshazzar is. Maybe the simple answer is, just someone else who cares about Demorest and speaks up in a witty way? With so much discontent in the public, I think that clever Belshazzar is the least we should be concerned about in the polluted social media waters.

On May 2, City Manager Kim Simonds was called to resign by Mayor Rick Austin and a petition on Change.org (490 signed; 500 signatures not received). A few of the comments were:

> "She's a child. If you don't give her her way, you're outta here. She's an embarrassment to the people of Demorest and women in power."

> "Really should call her Nancy Pelosi."

> "Mrs. Simonds has proven time and time again that she is incompetent, and her decision-making skills are pathetic at best."

> "We lived in Demorest for over six years, just moving to my husband's childhood home last fall. When Chief Krockum was appointed, our neighborhood was much safer as they patrolled regularly. Often it was Chief Krockum himself. He was involved and invested in our town and community. Ms. Simonds is an outsider who does not call Demorest her home and it shows. She does not have the city of Demorest's best interest at heart, only personal vindictives."

> "I am ready to see The City of Demorest thrive. I don't believe that is possible with the current City Manager or certain members of the council. This lady has proven that she cannot lead. She needs to go and so does Hendrix. Enough said...."

It breaks my heart seeing John's name out there in a negative light. People are free to exercise their right to communicate, their right to express the First Amendment. The concern is always for the tone being set though in the public eye.

Rick has a strong reputation for picking a fight with the LGBTQ community or really any ethnic community that is not of the white race. How far does his influence go? I will give you an example of something in the water in these parts. John and I invited a newly elected city council member to lunch. We were getting acquainted by showing each other our family photos. When I showed him a picture of Josh and his wife, Sukanya, a second-generation Asian American from India, the new councilman quickly asked, "She's dark! Where is she from?" Right at lunch!

In addition, we've known our attorney, Abe, for decades. His last name is "Sharony." Another councilman during a phone conversation recently said, after complimenting him as a "very sharp" attorney, "I noticed the name, *Sharony*. Is he *Jewish*?"

After a pause, I said, "Maybe."

Abe's late wife, Barbara, had given me an easy recipe for light and fluffy matzo balls, which I make frequently. I know he was from Romania, but his origin never even came into my mind though. He had handled many of our family's legal matters over the years. From that point, two days after his ethnicity question, Abe was coming into town from Atlanta, about ninety minutes away, to attend a city council meeting. Now, I feared what may be said in front of him! In fact, Abe is fluent in Hebrew, Romanian, French, and Spanish. Wouldn't it be quite the show if he spoke in a "foreign language?" On top of his law practice, Abe teaches ethics at Emory University and has been horrified by the unethical behavior he has witnessed from the mayor and his attorney buddy.

Sometimes reason goes out the door in these public forums as if it's another private chat over coffee. Rick, who lives in Demorest, had made a statement in a public meeting that he was sexually molested twice as a child growing up here. He was presiding over this meeting.

Recalling Reputation

As of this writing, critics have raked up enough support in the form of 1.6 million signatures to push for a recall election of California's Gov. Gavin Newsom. Though I am neutral concerning Gov. Newsom and obviously I'm more concerned about my own city councilmen, the very nature of a recall turns my stomach because it signifies wrongdoing, contempt, reputational damage.

News made it to neighboring Clarkesville that former Demorest City Councilwoman Florence Wikle made good on her promise to pursue recall of John *and* Nathan. In addition, a newly formed group in Concern Citizens of Demorest (CCD) was simultaneously pursuing recall of Mayor Rick Austin.

"I issued three recall applications yesterday—for Nathan Davis, John Hendrix and Rick Austin," said Habersham County Elections Supervisor Laurel Ellison on Tuesday. "Florence Wikle requested the two applications for Nathan Davis and John Hendrix, and the Concerned Citizens of Demorest Inc. requested the one for Rick Austin."

I couldn't believe that John and Rick were being compared to one another in some shameful way.

Florence Wikle is credited for sparking an investigation into missing funds totaling $600,000 between 2009 and 2013 under Mayor Malcolm Hunnicutt and former City Manager Juanita Crumley. Mayor Hunnicutt had refused to take a lie detector test, which I find disturbing. The findings concluded that financial procedures at the time were too intricate, possibly masking theft, and the leadership of Hunnicutt and Crumley only underscored the suspicious activities. Hunnicutt, who died in September of 2020, had served as our mayor for thirty-nine years and accomplished numerous respectable milestones for our city.

Alongside John's father, Hunnicutt was influential in establishing the Demorest Water System throughout the rural areas of Habersham County. For $600,000 to vanish under his watch is alarming. Despite audits and the Georgia Bureau of Investigation's efforts, the missing funds is still a whodunnit. Needless to say, Wikle was my hero, too, for exposing the truth—before her treatment of John, another crusader for truth.

According to Georgia law, a public officer can be recalled at any time during his term or office except during the first 180 days or the last 180 days of his term.

Wikle and other citizens were outraged when Kim had removed Police Chief Robin Krockum and tried to replace him with his predecessor, Chief Greg Ellingson. But Krockum had been reinstated and reached a settlement for $20,000 with the city. The issue gave birth to vicious rumors that got touted as facts.

Official sponsors are the electors who circulate or file an application for a recall petition who were registered and eligible to vote in the last general election or special election for the office held by the public officer to be recalled and must reside in the electoral district of the officer sought to be recalled.

"They need to get 100 signatures for Nathan Davis and John Hendrix and 94 signatures for Rick Austin," Ellison said.

Grounds for recall are that the officer committed an act or acts of malfeasance while in office, has violated his oath of office, has committed an act of misconduct in office, is guilty of a failure to perform duties prescribed by law, or has willfully misused, converted or misappropriated public property or public funds entrusted to or associated with the elective office.

As the coals of corruption were heating up in the fire pit, our attorney, Abe, asked John if he would just consider resigning.

In his most heartfelt phrasing (and I promise, I didn't help him with this one!), John replied:

> "Sadly, only seven months into my job as a councilman, I have both observed and experienced the treacherous tactics that are ruthless, deceiving, and self-serving from one city official to another which hindered the progress of the city's administration.

> "I am going to be candid with you, the citizens of Demorest rely on us, the council, to govern. The council members are expected to be guided by the Charter, to set aside any personal agenda, to work as a team, and to do what's best for this city, not just for yourself and/or certain individual.

> "After the May 5th meeting, I was encouraged by the overwhelming support from our Demorest citizens, most of whom were unable to participate in the meeting due to their age and the Governor directive of "shelter in place." Most comments from them were 'Don't give up.' 'We are with you.' 'We voted for you, not those trolls who don't live here.' 'Stay, we appreciate your integrity.' 'Demorest needs you.'

> "So, NO, I am not going anywhere."

"Shelter in place" was a scary phrase reminiscent of the Cold War when people did duck-and-cover drills to prepare for a nuclear attack, but to John, giving up and allowing vultures to take over our city was scarier. We could handle the shelter in place; we couldn't handle abandoning the fight for what's right.

As I've described, some citizens thought along the same lines enough to take action. Concerned Citizens of Demorest Inc. formed on June 8, 2020, shortly after Kim called for Joey Homans to step down, by Deborah B. Showalter and Teresa M. Benischeck. Showalter had been openly critical of Austin in the past, questioning whether a conflict of interest existed because City Attorney Joey Homans previously represented Austin in non-city matters.

"Since 2014, our citizens have had their taxes reduced six years in a row,"

Rick retaliated in a statement to *Now Habersham*. "Our citizens have watched as we put every measure possible in place to ensure that every penny is accounted for. The city is now in the best financial shape that it has ever been, reducing debt by millions while equally growing our reserves. Our public works and public safety departments have become some of the best in the state, ensuring that we are well prepared, and our residents are well cared for … all while lowering taxes."

Rick went on to the discuss the group attempting to recall him. "Members of the Concerned Citizens of Demorest are citizens, and they are evidently concerned. Given our accomplishments as a city, people should ask them what actually concerns them. They are a small, vocal group whose actions are politically motivated and not in the best interest of our city. Further, as a nonprofit organization, they may be stepping well over the federal IRS guidelines regarding political, disparaging activities."

The press painstakingly outlined the guidelines of a recall, lengthening the breaking news, but John was the subject of two recalls within six months, which was thought to be prohibited. I share the guidelines here for education purposes—you never know when your city could be tricked!

The application for recall must be submitted for verification within 15 days after issuance.

Along with the signatures, the application must contain a statement that the officer for whom recall is sought has, while holding public office, conducted himself or herself in a manner which relates to and adversely affects the administration of his or her office and adversely affects the rights and interests of the public and stating the appropriate ground(s) for recall as set forth in the Georgia Public Officers Recall Act of 1989, with a brief statement of the fact(s) upon which the ground(s) are based.

One of the sponsors must be designated as chairperson, who will represent the sponsors in all matters pertaining to the recall process.

According to Georgia law, within four days after the application is submitted for verification, excluding weekends and legal holidays, the public officer to be recalled may petition the superior court in his county of residence to review the sufficiency of the grounds for recall and the facts asserted in support of the grounds for recall. If enough signatures are verified on the petition for recall, a recall petition will be issued.

A recall petition must contain signatures equal to 30% of the active voters registered and eligible to vote at the last preceding election for the office of the person for whom recall is sought. Circulators will have 30 days to submit the petition.

Within five days after the election supervisor has certified the legal sufficiency of a petition, he or she shall immediately notify the municipal election superintendent, who issues the calls for the recall election. If a recall election is called and more than

50% of those voting cast ballots in favor of the recall, the office is immediately vacated.

Georgia law specifies that a special election to fill any vacancies created by a recall election must be called within 10 days after the recall election and must be conducted not less than 30 nor more than 45 days after the date of the call.

State law allows the person who is recalled may run in the special election to fill the vacancy. If the official resigns prior to the holding of a recall election, no recall election will be held, and the vacancy will be filled in accordance with state law. Should a recall petition be found to be insufficient, no further applications for recall can be issued for six months from the date of the finding of insufficiency.

If a recall election fails to recall the public official, no further application for recall petition can be issued for six months from the date of the recall election and all pending applications and petitions are void.

I had a hard time believing that Florence Wikle, or anyone for that matter, was inspired to recall John, who is so good-natured. He doesn't believe in arguing or being aggressive with people. Even in defending himself, he feels like it's a small town, where everyone knows him—that "they" didn't *deserve* to be confronted. He didn't want to go against anyone even if they did something wrong to him. Until he got recalled. Until he got recalled twice. He couldn't bear that under his family name. Everyone knows the family name and of his father's legacy in Habersham County.

One late night, John wasn't doing any favors for his own weary eyes as he sorted through dozens of emails. In the next room, I heard him draw in breath. It wasn't a good sign. He had enough.

As I approached him, rubbing my own eyes, John stated, "Let's talk to Abe about defamation and the frivolous recall."

Defamation is the action of damaging the good reputation of someone. John needed to defend himself.

We brought Abe in for legal counsel on the recall and the defamation. Abe went with John to an executive session the first time after the lawsuit and they all wanted to know why sharply dressed Abe was in attendance again.

Joey, the city attorney, said arrogantly, "You can send us an invoice and the city will cover you for the lawsuit, whatever representation you have to make."

Abe replied, "John didn't hire me for this lawsuit. He hired me way before. This lawsuit is only a sidebar. I'm here to sue for defamation and the recalls against John."

Silence sharpened the otherwise plain beige room. Then Rick immediately piped up with, "Oh, I had nothing to do with that!"

But he *had* personally called for the resignation of John and Nathan twice, then the recall application produced only a fraction of signatures that were required. The paperwork didn't contain the basics. The people who supplied the notary stamp was not supposed to be on the signature page either, yet one of them had her name on the same page to balloon the numbers.

Ironically, the person who had filed the first recall ended up contracting COVID-19 while trying to solicit the damning signatures, the scarlet letters for John to wear, from our neighbors.

Chapter 7

FIRE! ... AND OTHER LINE ITEMS

"The mind is not a vessel to be filled but a fire to be kindled."
—Plutarch,
Philosopher

I wish I didn't know all there is to know about firetrucks, a highly specialized topic, but I swear I do. Do a quick search of the news in Demorest, Georgia and you will, too, from the types of engines, how much water they hold, and the different signals for *fire* and *rescue*, to how long it takes to build a truck and how long they last.

A firetruck was originally budgeted in the SPLOST (Special Purpose Local Option Sales Tax) fund, a popular method for financing needed capital projects via an optional one percent county sales tax used to fund capital outlay projects proposed by the county government and participating qualified municipal governments. The budget in August 2020 for a new firetruck was $580,000 and before that, the fire chief asked for $650,000. We had to fight like crazy to get $20,000 or $30,000 off.

As soon as the $580,000 was approved, Kenneth Ranalli, who has respectably been the fire chief for a decade, brought in a proposal for $650,000. The city treasurer, Joely Mixon, CPA, city attorney and Rick all recommended this quote of $650.000. All council members were against this. The normal procedure is "open bid." No, the fire chief brought in one bid and the mayor recommended it. Then the treasurer concurred against the whole council. This consortium is out of Galveston, Texas to then get a firetruck built in Wisconsin, who has a dealership here. The mayor wanted to buy that truck from the beginning and has been pushing ever since.

They are tricking the whole community. On the matter of the firetruck, I couldn't take it and pushed John to debate this $70,000. It's common sense. When you have a budget, you don't look for a purchase that goes over that budget. If I budget $500 for shopping in Paris, I'm not going to set out to spend $750. Elected officials need to vote on major purchases like this, and it's kind of unheard of to keep stretching budgets by tens of thousands of dollars.

It may have been the fire chief who made the comment that "$125,000 had been coughed up for a dump truck that was not budgeted, so why can't we spend $650,000 on a firetruck that can turn on a radius, go up steep hills, protect our citizens, and last twenty years?" He even offered to apply some of his salary.

Kim replied, "We have two firetrucks. We didn't have a dump truck and couldn't function without it."

You would think with a small town, a mayor can be an upstanding leader and set the tone for the rest of council. No. He strives to get the most from the city, suck it dry, with the treasurer's help, and the water, $32 million worth of assets, can go to equity. Why are we $10 million in debt? Budgets for the police department and fire department total $1.5 million. Other towns of our size do not have a fire department.

The way I understand the law, the counties are responsible for protecting cities only if they are paid for that protection. In neighboring Statesboro, home to a large university of 24,000, the city takes care of all the students and residents with a separate fire service.

The most bizarre aspect of this battle for a firetruck for a full year is after trucks for the larger costs were turned down, the issue—and with larger price tags—would repeatedly come up again for a vote. It's completely nonsensical, and I am mystified by this. Demorest is in Habersham County, which has a fire department. If the truck doesn't work, a call goes to every department in the county for a truck.

Meantime, more proposals for high-priced firetrucks came in just before Christmas. We definitely needed Santa to gift us some water to put this freaky fire out.

I have February 2020 correspondence from Kim for context of this year-long battle for a firetruck:

> "Several weeks ago, one of our firemen backed the firetruck into a dirt bank. Ken is asking to get the truck repaired. Attached is the quote (over $11,000.00) and a photograph of the damage. His email is partly to convince me that he really needs a new truck—something he's wanted for quite a while. This is the third accident with a fire truck within the last twelve months. The other two accidents both happened when firemen were driving the fire truck TO LUNCH. They were not on calls. I asked that the fire trucks not be taken out of the truck bays unless they are on a call, and I was told they *must* be driven every day to keep the motors in condition."

The council voted against the purchase of the firetruck again and again.

They have six years to use that SPLOST fund to purchase a truck. Councilman Jim Welborn decided to chase down his own quote. I knew his reveal would be interesting. Jim is a builder and realtor and bi-vocational pastor at Pleasant Hill Baptist Church in Cornelia; he ran for mayor against Rick Austin in 2017.

As reported in *The Roar*, the student newspaper published by Piedmont University, Jim said he wanted to explore ways to promote small businesses, to have a less intrusive government, and to bring back a small community feel to Demorest.

"It's time to bring back a different balance, a balance that we used to have," he stated. "We used to be more of a small hometown, more friendly. There's more of a cold feel about Demorest, somewhat of an angry feel about that money-missing situation."

Jim was referring to money that went missing from Demorest City Hall between 2009 and 2013, before Rick took office. It was this scandal that led Austin to run for mayor in the first place, he has been known to say. "Every penny has been accounted for since I became mayor," Rick stated to the paper. "We've fixed a lot in the last four years. We've had clean audits, balanced budgets, efficient operations."

As is custom, Jim set out to obtain three quotes. Two were higher all the way toward $692,000. His final quote, including financing: $450,000.

When Jim revealed this at the meeting in February 2021, I couldn't help but fixate on Rick, who was red-faced once this number rolled out into the air. This raging fire did not seem to go out during the whole meeting. Why? Wouldn't it be a cause for celebration that the city could save so much money *and* have its new, shiny firetruck?

In April of 2021, in another baffling move, the council voted to keep the fire department outside of county hands. If you think about saving $250,000 or $300,000, it would have reduced the city's debt. Demorest has Piedmont University and a hospital. Why can't the city share the responsibility of all these citizens with the county that benefits financially from these two major entities? This is pure common sense for a municipal government.

I had come to understand why John decided to vote against the fire merger with the county, "the county failed to convince me why the amount of annual merger cost of $250,000 was doubled from the previous proposal of $125,000 last year," John passionately explained, "besides, the city may be able to effectively restructure the fire department, still keep our firemen, and save more than what the county offers. It's good if we can work with the county, but my job as a councilman is to protect the city's interest first."

The hot plot thickened when the VP of Fearless Flames showed up to present his case to the council. *The Northeast Georgian's* lead statement accompanied a picture of Nathan seeming like he was going to fall asleep, and I don't blame him since this topic is pretty tired! "Demorest City Council came face-to-face Tuesday with Chuck Miller, Vice President of Fearless Flames, the Marion Body Works fire truck..." What they didn't report is that Miller had brought a flask to the meeting, which he set down on his seat in the back of the room before approaching the council to defend the higher cost of the Marion truck.

Chapter 8

CLASH OF THE TITANS

*"Learning is not attained by chance; it must be
sought for with ardor and diligence."*

—ABIGAIL ADAMS,
U.S. FIRST LADY

JUST WHEN I thought things couldn't get worse in our fine Southern
city, Piedmont University, his very employer, had demanded the
city oust Mayor Rick Austin for conflict of interest.

These feuds have simply been nonstop—and in the haze of
nationwide divisions, an uproar for social justice and police reform,
and a deadly pandemic. No rest for the weary.

Then the real clash happened.

Piedmont University accused the City of Demorest and some
of its officials of fraud, racketeering, conflict of interest, breach
of contract, and deprivation of equal protection, calling for the
removal of Mayor Rick Austin and his firing as a tenured professor
at the college.

In a nine-page letter to Rick and other city officials, Piedmont
University attorney Patrick W. McKee of Newnan laid out allegations against Austin, City Clerk (now City Manager) Kim Simonds,

City Treasurer Joely Mixon, and others. The attorney letters are posted online in their entirety. All of the county publications didn't hesitate to publish them either as if to heighten the flames.

This is a red county. We honestly do not need any more fire!

"The demand letter accuses the city and individuals of misconduct that the city deems unfounded and without a factual basis," said Demorest City Attorney Joey Homans.

In his response to an Open Records request for the demand letter, Homans provided copies of documents, including legal advertisements for public hearings and minutes of public meetings where the rate changes were discussed, related to the water and sewer rates approved by the Demorest City Council in December 2018. Homans also provided correspondence about a building permit for the new Piedmont College Conservatory and documents related to Massachusetts Boulevard, located between the college's new conservatory and Demorest Springs Park. Lastly, Homans included documents about the Piedmont College Police Department, which was a point of contention in the college's allegations of extortion by the city.

McKee's lengthy letter to city officials was copied only to Piedmont College President James Mellichamp and Piedmont College Chairman of the Board Gus Arrendale, not the full Board of Trustees. In that letter, McKee named the City of Demorest, Austin, Councilman Sean Moore, as well as Homans, Mixon and Simonds. The allegations also took issue with the actions of Demorest Police Chief Robin Krockum, which the letter alleges were at the direction of Austin.

Here is an abbreviated version of McKee's letter, outlining the allegations, with supplemental info reported by *AccessWDUN*:

Deprivation of Equal Protection under the Fourteenth Amendment

- An "unreasonable hike in water and sewer rates against the college,

- "The 2019 water and sewage rate scheme serves no rational basis",

- "Beginning in the Fall 2018, the City of Demorest— including, in particular, Mayor Austin, Treasurer Mixon and Clerk Simonds— revised water and sewage rates to be implemented in 2019," noting those rate changes are aimed at Piedmont College, "a class of one."

Fraud

"Mayor Austin and the City of Demorest also have engaged in fraud against the college," McKee's letter asserts, referring to Austin and Mixon stating publicly that the city's water and sewer rates should be increased to offset the increased cost of providing services to the college, a tax-exempt entity.

RICO

"Mayor Austin and the city are not only guilty of fraud and Equal Protection violations against Piedmont College, but these claims are part of a larger conspiracy by the city and its officials against the college which constitutes racketeering through a government enterprise in violation of the Racketeering Influenced Corrupt Organizations (RICO) Act," the letter states.

That alleged extortion involved public hearings held by the city, in which Austin advocated closing Massachusetts Boulevard to expand the adjacent Demorest Springs Park and add parking for that facility; Krockum's statement that college police officers who were not certified would be arrested for impersonating an officer, which McKee asserts was an effort to force the college to contract with the city for its security; and by "devising a targeted, fraudulent water and sewage rate scheme that violates the college's constitutional rights and Georgia law."

Conflict of interest

"Rick Austin is in conflicting positions as mayor of Demorest and professor of biology at Piedmont College," McKee's letter states. "Rick Austin took office as mayor of Demorest in January 2014. Rick Austin also has been employed by the college as a full-time employee since 1997. As mayor, Rick Austin has introduced and voted on countless measures that directly deal with the college.

"Mayor Austin's public record discloses a strong personal bias against the college that he has used his public position to avenge," McKee's letter states.

Breach of contract

"Mayor Austin's conduct shows a regular pattern of negative bias toward the college, and this interferes with his obligations as a college employee," McKee's letter states. "This policy provides that a tenured faculty member may be terminated when the faculty member's conduct is found to be 'seriously prejudicial to the college'. Because Mayor Austin has been allowed by the city and the city council to use his position in a manner that directly violates the city charter to the significant detriment of the college, the college will seek resolution of Mayor Austin's contract with the college as part of any litigation with the city."

While alleging harm, fraud and extortion, the demand letter calls for the removal and termination of Austin in lieu of further legal action by the college against the city.

McKee's letter dated August 7 gave the city thirty days to take action to the college's satisfaction. "We are providing you with this notice to allow the city and its officials an opportunity to resolve these claims without incurring the time and expense of litigation," McKee's letter states. "However, if the college is unable to resolve these claims to its satisfaction within 30 days of your receipt of this letter, we reluctantly will pursue whatever legal remedies are available. We are providing you with this notice in the hope that resort to our legal remedies will not be necessary."

According to some local residents, all thirty-six board members for the college came from different parts of the country and voted to issue this lawsuit, which officially spans thirty-eight pages. The college lawyer has been working on this case for fourteen months. He drives a flashy sportscar and you see him driving around collecting information and working at my friend, Lawrence's café. For them to be that prepared, I know they are very serious.

Four months later in December 2020 before Christmas, John was outside putting up Christmas lights. I heard his phone rang in the front porch. A few seconds later, he rushed in with anxious look on his face. "It was John Popham on the phone. He was just served a lawsuit from Piedmont and needed to have a copy of the lawsuit made…I volunteered you." While copying, I noticed that the complaint was against the City of Demorest, Rick Austin, Bruce Harkness, Joey Homans, Sean Moore, John Popham, and Florence Wikle. It is apparent that no settlement has been reached since the August demand letter from Piedmont.

A hearing for Summary Dismissal and the writ of quo warranto took place on June 8. No order from the court has been issued yet. However, after the June 8 hearing, an attempt to a mediation suggested by the mayor's quo warranto attorney has been rejected by the Piedmont University.

Chapter 9

ALL EYES ON GEORGIA

"Fame is the thirst of youth."

—LORD BYRON,
POET AND POLITICIAN

WALKING ON THIN *ice.* That's what I think of when I ponder the tough winter of 2020 and lots of toxicity blanketing the city with the snow.

While I was contemplating everything going on in the world and when things would improve, I read the same-day notice of "Tree Lighting in Demorest City Square featuring Demorest Baptist Church, lighting of the Christmas Tree and Santa arriving on the fire truck," and Rick's angry response for not being notified sooner. Was this speck of much needed holiday spirit really something to be *angry* about?

Then John received an email from the city manager that she was infected with COVID-19. They don't believe in wearing masks in these parts! In fact, every city council meeting has been filmed and made available to the public online; you will see all council members wearing masks while our manly mayor never did.

A few days before Christmas, Representative Terry Rogers

requested use of the pavilion in the parking lot of our post office, in order to host U.S. Senator Kelly Loeffler and former UN Ambassador, Nikki Haley, two controversial figures in other parts of the country. About 250 attended.

The first quote by Sen. Loeffler posted was, "The radical agenda of the left, the abortion on demand, the taxpayer funding of abortion they want. We have to stop that. That's not right." *Meh.* Here, I will just say that the municipality should not be involved in political parties or take sides publicly.

Candidly, we are registered as independents anyway, which is probably no surprise to anyone. And yes, we wear masks to help control the spread of a pandemic that is deadly. We are not disease deniers.

At this time, Taiwan, my birthplace, was among the world's top in the way of safety measures for COVID-19. They "only" lost seven people at one point that I checked in the winter of 2020. A pilot was fined $10,000 for not abiding by safety measures handed down by the health department.

John is a physician. Josh is a surgeon. He and his wife had come home on my seventy-second birthday thinking we could gather outside and be safe. I thought we might avoid COVID-19, but we may die of pneumonia! Next thing we know, three outdoor heaters were delivered in time to have a nice, warm Christmas, courtesy of our son, Josh. We had a great time. Josh was paranoid, urging me to wash my hands every time I get up from my seat.

Amidst the pandemic, Chateau Elan smartly undertook a stunning renovation and made the restaurant in the atrium very safe in an immense space. That is the only place we did indoor dining for a year since most of the locals thought the pandemic was a hoax. With world leaders calling it "a little flu" (Bolsonaro in Brazil) and the illness of "one person coming in from China" (President Trump in the US), John and I were contemplating relocating abroad if this nonsense continued. Alas, John's council position didn't allow for it. Neither did his principles. We would have had "four more years" of battles between right and wrong nationally and locally. I lost fifteen pounds during this time period. With COVID-19, so many people gained weight eating and drinking more alcohol. These months were the worst we've had in our whole life. Every day. Stressful inbox.

Atlanta City Council is nowhere near here, which is entrenched in small, countywide chaos. At one point, our house is surrounded by confederate flags. Every household contains this paraphernalia. They tolerate John because he grew up here, the neighbors are friendly, but I'm still the outsider after decades.

Evangelist Charles R. Swindoll once said, "10% of your life is what happens to you, but 90% of your life is how you react to it." Guided by this belief, I have shrugged off countless discriminative remarks and reversed many unfair treatments to my advantage over the last five decades. This is America, the country I love, better or worse, I am part of it and will stand by it. Likewise, Demorest is where John and I live. Our loyalty to this town is unconditional. We want to do what's best for our city.

I could play the race card every day. So could Fire Chief Ranalli's wife, who is also an Asian American. Let me tell you why we're not more intimate with each other. The chief brought her and their young daughter to John's office right after John won the election, given I am the only other Asian American woman within the city limit and the councilman-elect's wife.

She beamed as soon as we were introduced, "You have such a nice lot! Why don't you give me a piece of it, and I can create a pond? We can have fresh fish every day!" Her eyes were wild with possibilities.

I tried to keep a straight face. John looked at me. I looked at John. Then she said that because her eyelids were droopy, she needed John to refer her for a surgeon to cosmetically repair her eyelid. All this wonderful substance in the form of favors and bold requests in about forty minutes. Asking me for a fishpond and maybe I get one or two in a month? I was told that if you go to her house, you may see chickens in the yard, too; that "everything under the sun" is growing there. This is simply not my approach to bonding with someone. This interaction took place the second week after John was elected. The fire chief wanted his budget endorsed and to be sure his job was secure. I believe he was making his rounds to the new council members.

Our son, Josh, will not return to Demorest. He's in a town two hours away and wants us to move closer. We're experiencing a lot of statewide tension though so neither of our households are immune, however.

Gov. Brian Kemp signed a massive overhaul of election rules passed by the Republican-controlled Georgia legislature that enacts new limitations on mail-in voting, expands most voters' access to in-person early voting and further inflames the state's debate over voting rights.

The ninety-eight-page bill makes dramatic alterations to Georgia's absentee voting rules, adding new identification requirements, moving back the request deadline and other changes after a record 1.3 million absentee ballots overwhelmed local elections officials and raised Republican skepticism of a voting method they created. "With Senate Bill 202, Georgia will take another step toward ensuring our elections are secure, accessible and fair," Kemp said in a live-streamed speech. "Ensuring the integrity of the ballot box isn't partisan, it's about protecting the very foundation of who we are as Georgians and Americans."

The intervention of the CEOs from Atlanta-based giants, Coca-Cola and Delta, among many nationwide, is a sign of success for the pressure campaign by Democrats and civil rights groups in Georgia, now a critical "swing state." Joe Biden became the first Democrat since 1992 to win the state, which was also responsible for handing his party control of a 50-50 Senate in two run-off elections in January.

Chapter 10

UNMEASURED VICTORY

"Luck is where opportunity meets preparation."

—Seneca,

Orator

EVEN THOUGH THE winter was tough, we remained healthy, and the season brought a sense of renewal. I started working on this book, which is both an art and a science, and it was election time across the spectrum of politics, including our municipal government. It was time for John to use his position a bit more forcefully.

It is clear why city council needed to remove Joey Homans once and for all. But there was also the problem of Joely Mixon, whose behavior had not always been so overt.

In October 2020, though, she only gave two days for auditing the city. This same audit would have to go to Moody's for a rating. We cannot afford not to submit the report, or it would be another minus. The city manager was told to be in compliance to bring the rating up. Joey Homans and Rick were covering up for the treasurer. Both Nathan Davis and Jim Welborn said this city treasurer needed to go or the corruption would continue. John had learned from Kim that Nathan contacted the independent auditor, Joey

Kitchens, CPA, and asked why he resigned abruptly. Joely didn't tell us that she messed up. She refused and blamed it on the independent auditor. Kitchens was not going to say anything, but he was contacted about the timeline, so he felt he needed to reveal this to the council, as he is no stranger to negative relationships and conflicts of issue.

It was due to this incident that Nathan contacted John for the first time in over six months. He also apologized to John for throwing him under the bus with his May 1, 2020, press release that caused two unsuccessful recalls for John and him, and also caused John having to retain legal counsel to protect him. He said sincerely, "I was wrong for doing that, John. I am so sorry. I was given bad advice. Sorry for the pain I caused for you and Mei."

Later, John said to me, "Hopefully, he has learned the lesson. The councilmen need to work together for the city. I am willing to set all these aside and move on."

"I agree," I told John, "Except from now on, trust but verify."

An hour before the January council meeting, we were at Chicago's Pizza, a local spot. Nathan walked in and the waitress asked Nathan what he wanted to drink. He huffed with neuroticism, "Do you have whiskey?" They don't. Beer and wine only. And awesome deep-dish pizza.

I'm not sure the brown liquid would have been enough to quell Nathan's nerves. It was time to remove two of the three characters that had caused the city so much grief for the past several years. It was time to demonstrate our solidarity and in a public way, which Nathan was having trouble with. For me, this type of situation is business as usual (causing a stir or solving a problem)!

When Nathan was walking to the parking lot after, John followed him and insisted, "Nathan, everything will be all right. Tonight, we get rid of this city attorney, or he will never go."

Mustering up determination, he said, "I know. I'm going to do it. I'm going to do it." He was working himself up and standing tall. Did I even see him puffing up his chest in his polo shirt?

Nathan is very Southern, mild, gentleman-like and he's not accustomed to any confrontation. I was told that once he had been housed in a facility for protection from domestic violent from his ex-wife. It broke my heart to learn he had suffered abuse from his intimate partner, but this knowledge also helped me understand where he was coming from and how I might encourage him to display some grit when we needed him most. After all, he had taken public office, too, which carried tough decisions and exposure. Backbone needed!

Given the personality analysis, I want to believe that Nathan didn't mean any harm against John back in the spring when he threw him under the bus openly in the hungry press. I suppose time will tell.

John said, "We cannot have another year of this. What are you afraid of?"

"I'm afraid of what people will think of me."

I replied, "People are entitled to their opinions, but they do not own the truth. Sometimes you need to have thicker skin and not hold onto what people say. I'm seventy-two years old. You know what John and I have gone through. We're still here. If that's all we cared about, we would be six feet under. You're much younger than us. You have a bright future and political ambitions. Do not be discouraged by what people think, or you will never get anything in life done. You can't please all the people all the time."

After this conversation with me that did what it was designed to do—fire him up—Nathan had called John one night and shouted, "I'm ready. I'm ready to f**k them!"

From that point on, he was empowered. John complained, "But now he has this sour mouth. The *F-words* are being slung around everywhere."

I said, snickering, "Let him be. He is struggling with confidence and expression. Let him express."

Rescuing the City

In order to make a motion and vote for the whole roster of appointments for city council, including all department heads and contractors, an annual meeting is called at the beginning of the year. Normally, the mayor presides over this process and calls for a second motion. If no one seconds and the motion fails, he might not call for another motion. This task could last all night if initiated at the beginning. Our alternate plan was to have the executive session and then stick the renewals at the end. Put the city attorney last, at the bottom of the list.

Again, this mayor is always very masculine and authoritative, with little room to improvise. He is the opposite of agility. Well, John encouraged him to do a roll call with the appointments instead. Surprisingly, Rick agreed.

Joely Mixon was absent at the meeting that night. When her name came up, Rick, in his usual gruff voice and awkward manner, prefaced the vote with: "She started in 2015. This city didn't even have a credit rating, much less a bond rating. The reason that we are financially stable and sitting in a place where we've got over $1 million in reserves is because of largely her. The reason we paid down over $5 million worth of debt is largely because of her. She's an extraordinarily professional individual, and she's also one of the most polite and pleasant individuals I've ever met."

Shawn Allen, the newest council member, voted "yes" on every one of them in good faith because he didn't know otherwise. Everyone else voted "no" on Mixon and Homans. Shawn was astounded like he did something wrong. "I thought when the city manager recommended, I should vote yes?"

Joey Homans had no class. While Nathan was thanking him for his service, he stormed out the door after shouting that the treatment of Joely Mixon was "shameful." Several robotic figures in the audience repeated the word "shameful" as the door slammed.

Sometimes change goes hand in hand with the dramatic arts. That city council meeting was not easy for any of us. Rick's wife even attacked me! Once the reappointments of Mixon and Homans were dead, the mayor leaned back and said, "I don't understand. How did this all happen?"

His wife was sitting behind me on the right-hand side, and I heard her say,

"It's all because of the back-door meetings among the council."

I turned around to see who was saying that. She saw me turn my head and said, "And *you* were in there!" Just like that.

I replied, "Wait a minute. You make an accusation; that is false. You better have proof."

Then the mayor said, "You can direct comments up here."

I said, "The meeting is over."

He said, "The meeting is not over until I adjourn it. Thank you. Do we have a plan, council? You made your vote. You made your voice known."

He said, "Out of order," still addressing me.

"I was provoked by Mrs. Austin."

Jennifer Austin said, "It's Doctor Austin, thank you."

John said, "Yes, I've heard that many times before, too, thank you." Everyone laughed.

Mrs. Austin had earned her Ph.D. and wanted the world to laud her for it apparently. She's an elementary school teacher. I could have been nastier to say, "Well, I have seven doctors in my family. Medical, dental, *and* PhDs." I didn't want to call anyone else doctor. Here, she sounded just like her husband. This was a public meeting.

Did she really need to be called doctor? It was an embarrassment. Earning a Ph.D. did not prevent Mrs. Austin from exhibiting poor temperament. It's what I call "knowledge without character."

Abe was sitting two chairs down from me in the name of social distancing. We were in the front row, and he moved over next to me and whispered, "So happy to hear you speak up to her, Mei."

As a preface to what happened, the newspaper printed an extremely biased article on termination of these two contractors on January 5, 2021, in our annual reappointments. The part that is meaningful to me as a citizen that I knew they wouldn't print: Joey knew he may lose his job with the city, and he thought Rick could help him get through this. He sent an email to all councilmen a couple days before stating, "Here is the roster of renewal. If you have any questions, let's discuss these renewals before the council meeting." Well, this didn't need to be discussed. Discussion is not required. The appointments are either renewed or not.

Within days after the new councilmen taking office, John received a message with the attachment from councilman Jim Welborn, stating, "Rick wants the new councilmen to meet department heads alone."—and the attachment was the mayor's message to the two new councilmen:

---------- Forwarded message ---------
From: Rick Austin <rick.austin@me.com>
Date: Wed, Nov 11, 2020 at 4:38 PM
Subject: Orientation Meeting

Gentlemen,

First, congratulations on your victories! Well done to you both.

Second, would you please set aside some time next week to meet with department heads, Joely Mixon, and Joey Homans. While I understand that some meetings may have been scheduled for Mrs. Mixon and another councilman, I urge you both to meet with our professionals without other council or myself present.

This year has been a struggle. Government is difficult, particularly when first starting. There are numerous laws and procedures that govern our decisions and guide our processes. We have failed as a council (council includes me) in that regard more than a few times this year. All too often, the sound advice of our professionals have been ignored, leaving us in very difficult positions.

Would you please meet with our professionals without anyone else on council there? Their decades of governmental experience is worth listening to. This will give you both an unbiased and knowledgeable basis to help with decisions that must be made as a council member.

If you are amenable, please let me know your availability and I'll get them in contact with you.

I look forward to working with you both. All the best!

Rick
[phone #]
Rick Austin, Ph.D.

The message from the mayor speaks by itself. What he didn't know is that Jim Welborn was all for the city attorney and the city treasurer to go.

John had spent thousands of dollars of his own money to have our attorney present at this meeting, and my advice was to do what's best for the city—with a sparkling new year in front of us! Nothing else mattered but ensuring that city council could terminate negative relationships and remove toxicity. You couldn't put a price tag on this.

I was kind of offended when *Now Habersham* reported that our ousting of Homans and Mixon was "unceremonious."

The Northeast Georgian called the meeting "bizarre" and "contentious." The meeting minutes from that evening say it best in firetruck-red font: *No Second.* Meaning, there was no second vote or motion to reappoint these individuals. *Finally.*

Our attorney, Abe, was elated at the meeting though he didn't make a public display of his reaction. I think he was simply happy for John and the city. Abe is quite familiar with John's integrity. I'm not sure how much more sleep John and I could lose from having these unethical figures in positions of power tricking my city.

I didn't want to embarrass John. He's the one on the council! I will talk all day long as a citizen particularly when I'm attacked, however. We had one objective, and I didn't have to say another word. Rick took the bait. We had all been studying his crafty political tactics. He is always prepared with preemptive strikes. I advised, first off, don't react to what he says. Emails and such, because this is his way of trying to be prepared for a strike against everyone. In my view, he is a narcissist. I was proud of Nathan though. This act of justice meant a lot to him. John was going to resign. Nathan was going to resign. Instead, John called in Abe to give them encouragement and reinforce that John was doing the right thing. He said that attorney was walking on thin ice anyway and about to be gone based on unethical conduct. Kim had gone to the biggest law firm in Atlanta, the Denton Law Group, and they would not even use their letterhead to address the matter in writing. They didn't want anything to do with municipal musings.

We were inundated that night with positive phone calls and messages of support. They called the council members that voted no, "Three Musketeers."

The president of Concerned Citizens of Demorest was traveling in Florida and called at 10:00 after seeing the Facebook broadcast, beaming, "My husband and I are giving each other high-fives. We tried to get this done for years! We are going to supply you guys with capes, our superheroes."

Well, John replied not to move too fast on the capes and lassos because they needed helmets first—to protect themselves from the backlash.

"It's coming," he said. "It's coming. Don't celebrate yet."

Sure enough, two city planning commissioners, friends of the mayor I'm convinced, resigned. They wrote a letter to the council, stating that councilmen are "untrained, inexperienced and uneducated." These insults were repeated in the paper.

The mayor scowled that night, "What are you going to do? You don't have a treasurer and you don't have an attorney."

Kim said demurely, "I'll provide a list of replacements." I had expected her to be more enthusiastic. Her nemesis, Joey Homans, was gone.

Chapter 11

DISSENT VS. DECENCY

"Morals are private. Decency is public."

—Rita Mae Brown,
Novelist and Activist

Laughter is good for the heart, which beats about 115,000 times a day, so there is plenty of opportunity to improve its rhythm. So, what was so funny?

The firetruck debacle continued, as in a surprise move, the mayor brought in a lead teacher from the fire academy, with countless fire service certifications. In a tone of irritation, Rick framed the presentation with, "I have no idea what he is going to say. More information is better than not having information." It's never enough when it comes to this topic apparently. The gist of the information was the same: the E1 truck is an assembly-line truck of mass production whereas the Marion is customized from the ground up, "with love and care." He gave lots of dramatic pauses in order for his words to settle in before Rick thanked him for his time and the motion was made to vote on the firetruck *tonight*.

He addressed the council forcefully, "You can go over budget anytime you want. We didn't allocate $18,000 for PR services either, did we?"

Someone in the back of the audience coughed like a rat crawled in his throat. But the city council saw red for so long, they would not be distracted any longer. They voted to buy the E-1 firetruck! A version that will save the city $250,000.

Here's the punchline: Mayor Rick Austin refused to sign the lease-purchase agreement and went on the radio to say he would not sign it because he didn't agree with some of the features. The council had to go to the city attorney to force an ultimatum—sign or say goodbye—since he is the only one who can sign city documents tied to the city's finances. It was all so ludicrous, I let out a deep belly laugh.

Even with a new PR rep in place, for $1,500 a month, or the $18,000 Rick was referring to, which the council voted for to polish the city's reputation, our image is not being smoothed out with so many cats being rescued from trees.

To the city council's move to hire a PR agent, Rick confirmed with our new city attorney that "he" is the official spokesperson for the city. "If I had a vote, it would be a hard no. Our press is not our enemy. Over twenty years I've dealt with them, our press is our friends."

I suppose he would call the local press friendly! The mayor's advocacy is for his own opinion—he never agrees with the council. He imposes his will on the city. He is always countering the council. Then like wildfire, the discord spreads to brazen opinion pages and cover stories with headlines screaming conflict. It is like a brand-new era every time the paper reports that a city council was "relatively calm."

In this new year, John and I have been concentrating hard on decency over dissent, but the mean and ugly have too many places to run rampant.

When John stood up for himself against two recall acts, and had Abe draw up and circulate "cease and desist" letters, Rick said, "You're a public official and should be able to accept criticism."

This wasn't garden-variety criticism, however. Recalls, by their very nature, imply wrongdoing or lack of credibility; that you should not have been put in a position to represent the community in the first place. This is damaging to someone's image.

I couldn't believe the night that Ms. Recaller poked John's chest after the meeting. With her white hair in disarray and eyes popping out from inside drooping skin, she looked like she needed meds to wake up. Did she sleepwalk into the meeting? She had the audacity to demand an apology from John for sending a cease-and-desist letter to her home. John handled the situation like a gentleman and tried to keep the focus on his character that she was taking an ax to from her unsuccessful recall efforts. She didn't apologize.

He did get an apology from Florence Wikle's co-recaller, Amanda Crump Mason, a former city council candidate, who admitted that she had been angry enough at John to notify *Now Habersham* about the letter. John messaged her and said, "We're all here for the community. I accept your apology."

Still, reporter Matthew Osborn of *Now Habersham* sent John a text wanting to obtain info from the cease-and-desist letter, asserting, "It's open record." Statements from the letter have never been reported accurately, so I supply it in its entirety:

NOTICE TO CEASE AND DESIST AND DEMAND
FOR RETRACTION

Ms. Mason:

Please be advised that I have been retained by Dr. John
Hendrix to pursue any and all causes of legal action for

defamation, libel and slander, regarding statements made by you and others "tending to injure (his) reputation and exposing him to public hatred, contempt or ridicule" under Georgia law.

MY preliminary investigation has uncovered several false and malicious utterances made by you or attributed to you, including: the accusation that "Councilman Hendrix (has) been trying for a year to get rid of our city fire department," published on January 25, 2021, by nowhabersham.com; the similar Letter to the Editor attributed to you in the Northeast Georgian, on its face false and defamatory; and the mocking Facebook reference to "lovely councilman John Hendrix" posted by you on December 2, 2021.

Demand is hereby made that you retract the above referenced false and defamatory statements, and cease and desist, immediately, from any other false and defamatory statements regarding Dr. Hendrix.

By emailing a copy of this Notice to nowhabersham.com, we object to their publication of the above referenced false statement, showing reckless disregard for the truth, with no attempt to reach out to Dr. Hendrix for comment, and for violating their duty of fair and honest reporting. A retraction is also demanded from nowhabersham.com.

Descent

Does one ever get used to waking up to mass violence? Another mass shooting? I'm not the only one to notice how frequent this has become in the United States. It doesn't matter where you stand on the right to carry. Do you feel that a society of bloodshed is one that you want your children and grandchildren to inherit and follow by example? I do not.

When the mayor, who often carries two guns into city council meeting, proposed on the agenda that the council vote for Demorest to be a sanctuary city for the Second Amendment, I stopped laughing. Habersham County was already the first in the nation to become a "sanctuary county," which is the umbrella for every city in that county to follow suit. His agenda item was…well, overkill.

On March 16, 2021, a series of mass shootings occurred at three spas or massage parlors in the metropolitan area of Atlanta. Eight people were killed, six of whom were Asian women, I might emphasize, and one other person was wounded. A suspect, twenty-one-year-old Robert Aaron Long, was taken into custody later that day.

In the council meeting, Nathan was the first to respond, calling himself a "gun guy," but amidst stammering, which I presumed to be due to nervousness over the topic, which has a tendency to bring out the worst in people in this part of the nation, he made it clear that the mayor's request was fruitless and poorly timed. The council voted against it and Rick was furious. It was like fire radiated from his bald head.

Under federal law, you're prohibited from owning a gun if you've been: convicted of a crime punishable by more than one year in prison; convicted of domestic violence; subject to a restraining order for harassing, stalking, or threatening an intimate partner;

committed to a mental institution; addicted to a controlled substance; or dishonorably discharged from the military. Many people who fall into one of the above categories still own guns, however. The issue typically comes up in relation to domestic abuse, as many of the men who committed high-profile mass shootings in the past year previously had been accused of domestic violence. Key: Advocates for a national gun registry argue that registering every gun would allow law enforcement to remove firearms from those people who legally aren't supposed to have them.

Conversely, more than 400 municipalities in twenty states have now passed resolutions opposing the enforcement of certain gun laws passed by state or federal lawmakers. In other places, sheriffs say they won't enforce specific gun safety laws and firearm confiscation statutes.

When the council voted no to make Demorest a sanctuary city for the Second Amendment (which again, the county already does), Rick offered his impassioned comments, which was inappropriate. "Requirement of registry of firearms is violation of the Fourth Amendment. I'm not registering mine—it is an unreasonable search. I'm a legal person. We never have to talk about First Amendment and the communication devices and mechanisms invented in the past 250 years since our founding fathers wrote the Constitution."

Then as always, Rick ended the meeting with the ironic, cringe-worthy statement, "Any further business for the good of the people?"

Chapter 12

PLEDGE OF A PUBLIC SERVANT

"Stories are the single most powerful tool in a leader's toolkit."
—HOWARD GARDNER,
PSYCHOLOGIST

HOW DO YOU trick a city?

The municipality has no jurisdiction under the state. If you run into problems of corruption, if you call the Georgia attorney general, you receive a message that we cannot take the complaint if this involves a municipality.

Lawmakers need to take a second look. Demorest is not the only city to go through something like this. This is more like a cartoon! Beyond my imagination. Here, you can see the characters and the environment of these meetings.

I told John, "I wish we could videotape all of these shenanigans."

On that note, city council meetings are videotaped and online, but I'm talking about all the edges around core events. What goes on behind the scenes. The phone calls. The assembly line of emails about concerns and conflicts. People wouldn't believe what we have gone through with this while John just tried to do a good deed and give back. It was supposed to be a matter of not being in financial shape and a few numbers here and there. I didn't expect to find a corrupt regime embedded in this place of 2,000. No one wants to get involved. DA. FBI. GMA. You now see the full story that defined one year of city council.

We got rid of two of the legs of the wobbly three-legged stool. People are afraid to serve, but we need new voices and faces from which those voices rise to overcome this negative image created by a few bad seeds. The papers did their job of smudging the council. "City in turmoil." "Battle of Demorest." They didn't talk about the new parks or anything resembling beauty.

Over the course of six months, our legal bill was $23,000. It was worth our attorney sitting in some of these meetings representing justice, fairness, and balance.

If I didn't write this book (and plan for others), our story would get buried in bad headlines. As long as this is my home and one that carries our family name, I refuse to see Demorest going down in flames. It doesn't matter how much the truck to put out those flames costs. I'm not sure who will be driving the truck. The fire chief resigned, and rumor has it that he was working at a paid event at the Piedmont University while on duty at the city, took his firemen with him, and left the fire department unattended. Yet, the *Northeast Georgian* praised his ten years of hard work and made no mention of the fact that he was about to be fired. Worse than that, they named John and Nathan in the article despite the fact that Jim Welborn presided over the fire department and Jim was quite unhappy with the fire chief repeating COVID-19 violations, along with the fire truck purchase episode.

At 7:30 a.m., right after John reading the *Northeast Georgian* article and chewing on the words, I heard John on the phone a little too zealous for the hour. "Good morning, Mathew! Did I wake you up?"

The reporter answered, "Yes…" with a sleepy tone.

"Good! Now we can talk!"

Based on John's blunt opening, I knew he had lost his patience with all the media nonsense. Later the same day, John and Nathan confronted reporter Mathew Osborn face-to-face and demanded a retraction. A more peaceful article was published.

Trickery persists, but so does truth. Pursue it with all the fire inside of you.

References

Belshazzar. "Cookies!" Demorest City. May 15, 2020.
  https://www.demorest.city

Chan, Stella, and Kyung Lah. "Critics of California governor
  gather enough signatures to force recall election." CNN. April
  26, 2021.
  https://www.cnn.com/2021/04/26/politics/newsom-recall-
  signatures-california-governor/index.html

Change.org. "Remove the Demorest City Manager-Kim
  Simonds." *Robin Skelton.*
  https://www.change.org/p/demorest-city-council-members-
  and-mayor-rick-austin-remove-the-demorest-city-manager-
  kim-simonds?redirect=false

City of Demorest. "City Council Work Session." *Regular Session
  Meeting Minutes.* January 28, 2020.
  https://cms8.revize.com/revize/demorest//01.28.20%20
  City%20Council%20Mtg%20(Regular).pdf

_____. "City Council Public Hearing and Special Called
  Meeting." *Regular Session Minutes.* January 5, 2021.
  https://cms8.revize.com/revize/demorest//01.05.2021%20
  Final%20Minutes.pdf

Cottingham, Hadley. "Demorest council meeting gets heated
  over money, bonds and a letter." *Now Habersham.* February 7,
  2020.

https://nowhabersham.com/demorest-council-meeting-gets-heated-over-money-bonds-and-a-letter/

Davis, Nathan. "Demorest councilman admits to unauthorized meetings, actions." *Now Habersham.* May 1, 2020. https://nowhabersham.com/demorest-councilman-admits-to-unauthorized-meetings-actions/

Dukes, Page. "Piedmont Professor Faces a Challenger in Mayor Elections." *The Roar.* November 12, 2017. https://piedmontroar.com/6223/news/piedmont-professor-faces-a-challenger-in-mayor-elections/

Fearless Flames https://fearlessflames.com

Fowler, Stephen. "Kemp Signs 98-Page Omnibus Elections Bill." *GPB.* March 26, 2021. https://www.gpb.org/news/2021/03/25/kemp-signs-98-page-omnibus-elections-bill

Grant, Adam. *Originals.* New York, New York: Viking, 2016.

Hannum, Mark. *Become.* New York, New York: McGraw-Hill Professional, 2020.

Harari, Yuval Noah. *Sapiens.* New York, New York: HarperCollins, 2015.

Law Office of Patrick W. McKee, LLC. "Claims by Piedmont University Against the City of Demorest and City Officials." Letter file accessible online. August 7, 2020. https://d3q2l9ughecwdu.cloudfront.net/wp-content/uploads/2020/08/Piedmont-College-demand-letter.pdf

Moore, Rob. "Popham wraps up 44 years of service on Demorest City Council." *AccessWDUN.* December 22, 2019. https://accesswdun.com/article/2019/12/861844/popham-wraps-up-44-years-of-service-on-demorest-city-council

_____. "Separate recall efforts target Demorest mayor, council-
men." *AccessWDUN*. July 29, 2020.
https://accesswdun.com/article/2020/7/924031/
separate-recall-efforts-target-demorest-mayor-councilmen

_____. "Piedmont University attorney's letter demands removal
of Demorest mayor." *AccessWDUN*. August 20, 2020.
https://accesswdun.com/article/2020/8/930853/
college-letter-demands-removal-of-demorest-mayor

Now Habersham. "Harkness running for county commissioner."
Staff Report. February 22, 2020.
https://nowhabersham.com/
harkness-running-for-county-commission/

_____. "Demorest removes Homans, Mixon from office, delays
firetruck SPLOST firetruck." Staff Report. January 5, 2021.

Osborne, Matthew. "Demorest council votes out treasurer, attorney." *The Northeast Georgian*. January 8, 2021.
https://www.thenortheastgeorgian.com/index.php/local-news/
demorest-council-votes-out-treasurer-attorney

Pereira, Eric. "Documents filed for recall of Demorest officials."
The Northeast Georgian. July 18, 2020.
https://www.thenortheastgeorgian.com/local-news/
documents-filed-recall-demorest-officials

Purcell, Joy. "Hendrix Sends Cease and Desist Letters to
Constituents." *Now Habersham*. February 4, 2021.
https://nowhabersham.com/
hendrix-sends-cease-and-desist-letters-to-constituents/

_____. "Demorest City Manager asks city attorney to resign."
Now Habersham. May 1, 2020.
https://nowhabersham.com/
demorest-city-manager-asks-city-attorney-to-resign/

Rea, Paul. "Florence Wikle relieved by report on Demorest's missing money." *Now Habersham.* May 12, 2015.
https://nowhabersham.com/florence-wikle-relieved-by-report-on-demorests-missing-money/

Rick Austin Photography. "Politics and Candidates."
https://rickaustinphotography.com/politics-and-candidates/

Russell, Dale. "Demorest Mayor calls rehiring of fired police chief a 1st Amendment victory." *Fox 5 Atlanta.* May 7, 2020.
https://www.fox5atlanta.com/news/demorest-mayor-calls-rehiring-of-fired-police-chief-a-1st-amendment-victory

Shearer, Lee. "Piedmont College to be named Piedmont University in 2021."
Athens Banner-Herald. June 23, 2020.
https://www.onlineathens.com/story/news/education/2020/06/23/piedmont-college-to-be-named-piedmont-university-in-2021/114788284/

Souther, Lauren. "Nikki Haley and Kelly Loeffler campaign in Demorest." *Fetchyournews.com.* December 20, 2020.
https://fetchyournews.com/featured/nikki-haley-and-kelly-loeffler-campaign-in-demorest/

Stirgus, Eric. "Professor's ouster leads to lawsuit, allegations at Piedmont College." *The Atlanta Journal-Constitution.* April 11, 2019.
https://www.ajc.com/news/state--regional/professor-ouster-leads-lawsuit-allegations-piedmont-college/fCNJvYttilVRC1Ha5MsMRI/

Wolfe, Kris. "30 Characteristics of a Good Guy." *Good Guy Swag.* August 8, 2013.
http://goodguyswag.com/30-characteristics-of-a-good-guy/

Zapotosky, Matt. "This might be the most corrupt little town in America." *Washington Post.* March 5, 2016.

CPSIA information can be obtained
at www.ICGtesting.com
Printed in the USA
BVHW031448260821
615314BV00003B/578